READY FOR ANYTHING:

THE MAKING OF A CHANGE LEADER

Jeff Haldeman, Ph.D.

Program Director,
Organizational Change Leadership
Professor of Management

Webster University

cognella® | ACADEMIC PUBLISHING

Bassim Hamadeh, CEO and Publisher
Kassie Graves, Director of Acquisitions
Jamie Giganti, Senior Managing Editor
Miguel Macias, Senior Graphic Designer
Angela Schultz, Senior Field Acquisitions Editor
Michelle Piehl, Project Editor
Alexa Lucido, Licensing Coordinator
Chelsey Schmid, Associate Editor
Kat Ragudos, Interior Designer

ISBN: 978-1-5165-0520-3 (br) / 978-1-5165-0521-0 (pbk)

ACKNOWLEDGEMENTS

Those who have influenced my thought life, teaching, consulting, and writing can be delimited to a fairly small group. I owe most of my original insights—such as the focus on impasse as a catalyst for a change in mindset, organizational climate, or culture—to the creative muse. Characteristically, when I review topics that I am interested in, I find that my interest lies in viewing the topic or theme from a variety of angles. The author has to live with his subject for a period of time before it will yield up its richness to him. During that period of incubation, the subconscious mind plays with the topic in novel ways, subjecting it to various forms of knowing.

In this book, I get at organizational change leadership and the leaders themselves by active knowing in the rational, irrational, and non-rational modes. I have learned to appreciate these three modes by learning from masters: Consider Kierkegaard and his appreciation of fear and trembling in approaching Almighty God. We don't adapt to change through rational analysis. We adapt by walking through fear and fire. This is the irrational in man as he faces the unknown and unknowable. As we attempt to steer our organizations through change, we want to project-manage our way and bring the tools of rational analysis to bear. We want to manage risk and uncertainty! This is all to the good; yet Kierkegaard suggests that we cannot have faith in a desired future without taking a leap of faith. In that leap there is danger, fear, and courage. All the management techniques and tools won't take it away.

There is room here for rational models such as I learned from my instructors at the Department of Organizational Behavior, Case Western Reserve University. Suresh Srivastva, Ron Fry, and William Pasmore taught me how to think more analytically, and to apply innovative perspectives such as sociotechnical systems, task-oriented team building, and statistical modeling to the problems of organizational life. I owe them a debt of gratitude. Ph. D. program graduates Denny Gallagher and Rad Wilson taught me how to roll with the punches as my ideals and methods came up against the political realities of a first major consulting job.

There have also been masters of the non-rational, such as Joseph Chilton-Pearce and Ernest Becker, who invited me to contemplate the erosion of cultural certitudes and the insertion of death and mortality into our tidy mission-driven organizational lives. In the United States, in particular, we who consider ourselves denizens of the middle class and of a working age still live to get ahead, to compete in the marketplace. In higher education, our old market space is eroding, and we have not yet captured new markets. Acting as agents of change (or of the status quo) we attempt to lead. In doing so, we need rational, irrational, and non-rational methods of plumbing reality—the reality we have and the reality we seek. It all comes together when the hockey team is on the ice rink and the puck is slammed into the net. Goal! (or not). Even when we fail, we get up, learn from our mistakes, and do it all over again.

The academic program in which this book will be used is called the Change Leadership Stacked Certificates/M. A. degree. Scott McClure, Senior adjunct faculty and collaborator extraordinaire helped me to develop the three certificates: Foundations, Managing Teamwork and Communications, and Managing Complexity for Total System Results. I also want to acknowledge my department chair in the Walker School, Barrett Baebler. He supported me with release time from the classroom and his extensive knowledge of the curriculum development process. Barrett was a tireless collaborator.

This theme of change leadership is a life theme, which finally came together in both a book and an academic program. This book supplements and in some way completes that curriculum. I owe thanks to the members of the Change Leadership Program Faculty Curriculum Community for their ongoing commitment to the design and implementation of the new program: Scott McClure, Nicole Roach, Tom Ahr, Rebecca Ellis, Jane Kerlagon, Bill Rearden, Linda Nash, Staci Harvatin, and Patrice Daquin. They have taught me, once again, that change is hard, messy, and joyful; sometimes it seems to be non-existent, even when we're trying our hardest! The solution is stepping back, regrouping, acting responsibly, using everything you know, and being persistent.

My wife, Margaret Haldeman, was a helpful critic and has supported my writing since I began this project. Thanks, too, to Marybeth McBryan, who helped in the initial stages of editing this book. Michelle Piehl and Chelsey Schmid, my Cognella editors, worked tirelessly on my behalf.

Finally, my heart-felt thanks to Steve Werner, my colleague in Religion and the Humanities, and long-time friend. Steve pointed me to Cognella as a possible publisher, and here we are!

CONTENTS

FOREWORD

The theme of this book is "changing ourselves to face the dilemmas of external change." I will not focus on organizational adaptation to external changes. That has been adequately covered elsewhere. We as managers and employees must change if we are to effectively meet the dilemmas we currently face. Character is telling. Something akin to ongoing conversion is required to wake us up! Collectively, we suffer from a heart condition. There is something wrong with our consciousness. We need to change our point of view and change the way we experience reality in organizations. We should fight our conditioning and learn to see the organizational worlds around us differently so that we can act in surprising and spontaneous ways!

Each of the chapters of this book is built on the following structure:

1. An essay on a change-related topic
2. Short case applications
3. Self-discovery questions

The purpose of this book is to broaden your understanding and deepen your ability to act. I have made an effort to borrow interesting ideas and insights from diverse sources. It is best to view the enterprise of management holistically. Those of us who manage, teach, and write must go outside the boundaries of academic disciplines to bring relevance to the field. Even more, we must extend the boundaries of the field itself to include topics that may be broader in scope. We will be viewing organizations as living, breathing, growing, and dying organisms (Rothwell & Sullivan, 2005). Biology and other natural sciences have something to tell us about what we are able to achieve as managers. We will develop ad hoc notions about organizational life and processes. Most of all, and in the spirit of a rigorous management science, we will call our organizations, and our joint day-to-day creation of them, into question.

For the purposes of this book, I will be taking a radical, existential point of view. Just for the moment, we will assume that we are totally responsible for the reality we create (even when we feel most stuck and can't see to change it). I am not saying that organizational forces do not press in on us or that other people do not sometimes make life difficult. I am only suggesting that we suspend judgment on those elements. What will matter is how we ourselves think, perceive, and act.

INTRODUCTION
Why I Wrote This Book

Like other consultants, teachers, and managers, I have an interest in global and organizational change. These are practical matters, not just of academic interest. In fact, academic discussions of organizational development (OD) and transformation (my field) often leave me feeling flat and dissatisfied. In academia, it seems, we spend too much time analyzing our world and too little acting upon it for the better. On the other hand, our professional field of organizational development has rattled on about the cutting-edge for decades, yet failed to create a meaningful intellectual bridge between the lessons of consulting practice and the relevant academic disciplines.

Conceptualization is important, and I try to do a lot of it in this book. I am attempting to create a middle ground between dense theory and practical application, between arid models and case studies of successful change. I believe we can best see what is actually there in the world of organizations by temporarily suspending our use of dense conceptual frameworks and replacing them—for a time—with efforts to elevate our awareness and consciousness. What does this mean?

Awareness can be developed and consciousness deepened by detaching from the need to understand why something is occurring—for example, why does my boss always lose his temper?—and focusing on a description of the phenomenon itself as it appears in context. Sometimes, by willfully suspending our powers of analysis—not an easy thing to do—we begin to see the emergence of something fresh and new. The same could be said of our inner state. We analyze ourselves, our actions, and our motives, ad nauseam, because we are so very relevant to ourselves. Ask us to try to detach from our current self-image and most of us would stare incredulously: What do you mean, detach from my self-image? Impossible. Yet phenomenology, the precursor of all philosophy, suggests it is possible to understand human consciousness and self-awareness without subjecting the things that we perceive to cause and affect analysis. We can see, hear, touch, and sense things without asking how or why. For example, observing the aftermath of a lay-off, we might say, "There is a heaviness in this organization. You can feel it when you walk in the door. This is what it looks like…" or, in a meeting, "Look at that woman in the Board Meeting; she's tapping her fingers on the table and staring down into her lap." We haven't imputed any motives or made any judgments. We are describing what we see. Edmund Husserl,[1] the oft-quoted German phenomenologist makes a plea for us over-educated, know-it-all managers and academics to do just that in his imperative, "to the things themselves!"

---

1   Internet Encyclopedia of Philosophy, 2011, Phenomenological Reduction section, 4

We are all very smart; we know a lot. Sometimes we know so much that we cannot see the forest for the trees. Paradoxically, in an age of complexity, we suffer from a paucity of creative thinkers who can clearly see emergent phenomena in a fresh way. We are burdened by conceptual baggage. In the Knowledge Age, we are flooded with science and technology and thousands of professional journal discussions, which are frequently less relevant to the concrete, practical realities of organizational life. Higher Education flourishes! In contrast, in the management and behavioral sciences there is a serious gap between theory and practice. M. B. A. programs proliferate, yet our graduates lack the capacity for imagination. We might ask what has happened? Why is it that a country with all the resources of the United States seems to have lost the capacity for social innovation? I believe, and will argue in this book, that we have been done in by our own advanced knowledge frames and paradigms. We want to understand complexity and seem to have lost the capacity for fascination, awe, and majesty. We need to find a way to re-capture *Wonderland*.

The same thing may be said for Organization Development (OD). In its newest and most transformational context, change leadership, OD is the application of principles, models, and methods from a variety of social and behavioral sciences to help organizations achieve and maintain effectiveness in the face of turbulent global change (Cummings and Worley 20082). Our field has been in existence for approximately fifty years. By now, many executives and managers are familiar with current terminology: transformational leadership, strategic change, self-directed work teams, organizational transformation.[2] The list goes on... but these are only words. In reality, OD consultants and other leaders of change help their clients do two things: (1) Uncover what is intangible or unknown about the complexity we conveniently call organizations, and (2) use that knowledge to understand and control human processes and business outcomes in specific situations. All of these situations are made-up of (1) rational, (2) irrational, and (3) non-rational elements. Business schools frequently teach their students to deal with what is, or seems to be, rational. By artificially segmenting business and management knowledge into discrete disciplines, we are able to provide the illusion that all knowledge is rational and consists of specialized bodies. Implicit in that codification is an apparent truth that if you master all of this, you will be able to master the experience of managing. Organizations, of course, are composed of living people who are susceptible to irrational outbursts and behaviors. This will often mean behavior which is dominated by hidden feelings and motives and which is not normally subjected to human discourse. We don't talk about it; it isn't nice. Cartoon commentator and management

---

2   See Burns 1978; Cummings and Worley 2009; Worley, Hitchin, and Ross 1996

critic Dilbert notwithstanding,[3] M. B. A. programs do try to handle this topic with a course in Organizational Behavior (OB). Marketing courses allude to it as a part of advertising and consumer behavior. In either case, it is mostly not treated as the potential stick of dynamite that it is. I like to think of this as purposeful neglect stemming from the ideological prejudices of both corporate and academic communities: If we can't see it, it doesn't exist (corporate). If it is not theoretical and conceptual, it doesn't exist (academic). The irrational does not have a good name in these circles. Neither does the term non-rational. Non-rational knowledge is knowledge obtained by intuition. Intuition is direct knowledge of an object or phenomenon or cognition without having to think about it. It is an aha moment. One way to gain this insight or understanding is through an act of contemplation. In our action-oriented culture, non-rational modes of knowing and being are often seen as navel-gazing. In the East, they may contemplate or meditate for hours in an attempt to know the essence of an object. Should we pursue this strategy in the United States, we are understood to be wasting our time and may be subject to disciplinary action. In this book, I will argue that in a time of rapid change, successful managers will need to become intimate with all three forms of knowing. The management of change is becoming more difficult for other reasons as well. The old is breaking down and the new has not fully arrived. In such times, economic meltdowns, massive layoffs, or four mergers in five years occur. Change seems to manage us. This is only an apparent phenomenon. As I hope to show throughout this book, we are still in control.

Many of the early OD consultants were psychologists who brought models of mental health to the work place. Individual professionals focused on speaking and behaving authentically to open up organizations and get people communicating. This was during the cultural revolution of the late 1960s. There was little competition in the marketplace. Executives had become organization men and their ten-tiered organizations were full of bureaucratic dry-rot (Argyris 1970; Whyte 2002). Organizational cultures cultivated conformity and killed initiative. To this situation the consulting psychologists brought a breath of fresh air. Their models and methods were countercultural. They shared many of the values of the corporate middle class but also represented divergent values of social activism and alienation that drove them to challenge the prevailing management orthodoxy.

Perhaps the best known of these pioneers was Abraham Maslow (1999). Maslow developed a needs model of motivation with which all managers and business students are familiar. Self-actualization stood at the pinnacle of his pyramid. It was Maslow's concept for personal growth that transcended both

---

3 Adams, Scott. 2016. Retrieved from http://dilbert.com/search_results?terms=MBA+Programs

survival needs and the higher level needs of the personal self. To the extent that it went beyond egoistic achievement and the cultivation of self-esteem, self-actualization implied psychological transcendence. We were meant to continually evolve to become all that we could be (Maslow 1968, 71–72). Here was theory and research that pointed to men and women as something more than the sum of their competitive, aggressive, and security instincts. For organizational psychologists, whose values were typically more socially responsible and morality based than their corporate counterparts of the day, this was a wedge that could be driven into the corporate psyche. Maslow's results stood in stark contrast to the dehumanizing conditions that existed in many Fortune 500 companies of the time. If man was something more than a corporate creature, his potential contribution to both individual and organizational development could only be fostered by a new kind of manager.

The early direction of OD was to teach people to be authentic, open, and, by implication, "relatively free of the more distorting personal defenses which could interfere with day-to-day interaction and communication at work" (71–72). Personal and organizational effectiveness came from real dialogue between people who trusted each other and were willing to make themselves vulnerable (i.e., to risk being wrong).

Today, some consultants and many managers are convinced that this model of management behavior is naïve. It does not seem like the way to get ahead, and it may no longer be relevant in an age where speed, technology, and virtual organizations challenge the limits of our human adaptability. People doubt if we have the time for open, face-to-face communication, although we seem to have plenty of time for the tweet, the blog, and the Internet. When time is measured in nanoseconds, we are always looking for short- cuts. Our age would have us believe that the annual report reflects the underlying reality for individuals in organizations; that the numbers and graphs are more important than the reality of thinking, feeling human beings who stand behind the externals. The fact is that global competition does not guarantee the development or adaptability of any particular organization, no matter how good the numbers or graphs. People have to think and behave more effectively for personal and organizational development to occur. Executives are expected to lead this process. When they do, when they excel at it, the results are exhilarating. Yet even when they do not, the individual organizational actor has a critical role to play, no matter what anyone else is doing. In a very real sense, we are always masters of our own destiny.

This is the essential premise of this book: Human beings, being themselves and making responsible choices to think and act with integrity, can enrich the organizational environment and create a climate of greater choice for everyone. This is an existential approach because the onus is on individual decision and choice, not top management or the executive team. There are times when we have to go it alone. In matters of importance and concern, we cannot look to the organization or to management to give us permission. We may well discover ourselves partnering with others to bring new life and promise to our workplaces. We often achieve more through collective effort. Nonetheless, in some important sense, we are still alone. You will see soon see what I mean. In many ways, it is a creative and exciting place to be!

REFERENCES

Adams, S. (2016). Retrieved from
http://dilbert.com/search_results?terms=MBA+Programs

Argyris, C. (1990). *Overcoming organizational defenses: Facilitating organizational learning.* Upper Saddle River, NJ: Prentice Hall.

Blanchard, K. H. & Johnson, S. (1982). *The one-minute manager.* New York, NY: William Morrow.

Bridges, W. (2003). *Managing transitions: Making the most of change.* New York, NY: Da Capo Press.

Burns, J. M. (1978). *Leadership.* New York, NY: Harper & Row.

Butz, M. R. (1997). *Chaos and complexity.* Washington, D.C.: Taylor & Francis.

Carroll, L. (2010). *Alice in wonderland.* New York, NY: Tribeca Books.

Cooper, G. (2008). *The origins of financial crises: Central banks, credit bubbles, and the efficient market fallacy.* New York, NY: Vintage Press.

Cummings, T. G., & Worley, C. G. (2009). *Organizational development and change.* Mason, OH: Southwestern Cengage Learning.

Internet encyclopedia of philosophy. (2011). Retrieved from
http://www.iep.utm.edu/phenom/.

Intuition. (n.d.). *Merriam-Webster online dictionary.* Retrieved from,
http://www.merriam-webster.com/dictionary/intuition

Maslow, A. H. (1968). *Toward a psychology of being.* New York, NY: D. Van Nostrand.

Phenomenology. (n. d.). *Merriam-Webster online dictionary.* Retrieved from,
http://www.merriam-webster.com/dictionary/phenomenology

Rothwell, W. J. & Sullivan, R. (2005). *Practicing organization development: A guide for consultants* (2nd ed.). San Francisco, CA: Pfeiffer.

Sartre, J. (1956). *Being and nothingness.* New York NY: Gramercy Books.

Vaill, P. B. (1996). *Learning as a way of being: Strategies for survival in a world of permanent white water.* San Francisco, CA: Jossey-Bass.

Whyte, W. H. (2002). *The organization man* (First ed.). Philadelphia, PA: University of Pennsylvania Press.

Worley, C. G., Hitchin, D. E., & Ross, W. L. (1996). *Integrated strategic change: How OD builds competitive advantage.* Reading, MA: Addison-Wesl

Organizational Gamesmanship

This chapter focuses on our tendency to relinquish personal power in organizations by being tentative in our commitments to invest and to act to improve things. Mature, independent people, who are neither overinvested in their past nor over-committed to any too-specific future, are in the best position to approach their current organization with power and grace. They can stand in the middle, bestriding the colossus of organizational complexity like a hero. While many employees grow sour and others leap-frog over their responsibilities to embrace the next milestone in their career, the fully present actors are in the best position to be themselves, spontaneously and radically, because they are playing a different game. The game is organizational tai chi. Slowly, playfully, and purpose-fully they invade organizational space, moving to their own inner rhythm, acutely aware of the game-playing nature of organizations. These perceptions do not bog them down. They are able to see beyond the eternal games.

From this perspective, we must disbelieve what we see and hear, not taking it at face value. An example is those employees who say they are dissatisfied, yet refuse to do anything about it. They are hanging on to a worn-out word that no longer describes their reality. After a certain point, the individual who stays, even though originally dissatisfied, will become more satis-fied. Psychologists call this cognitive dissonance (Festinger 1957). In layman's terms, it means that people can only tolerate discrepancies between their intentions and their actions for so long. At some point reality will intrude to correct the misperception. This is important to know, because it helps all of us to avoid the twin pitfalls of over- or under-reacting to the views of self and others we see in the workplace. What people say is not necessarily what they mean. If we were able to tap the rich, experiential reality that all of us carry deep within us, beneath the defenses, distortions, and self-justifications, we would be able to see who we really are. In the meantime, most of us dissemble (at least some of the time).

The Cost of Commitment

To obtain committed employees is the desire of every manager worth his salt. Yet what exactly is commitment? If we feel emotionally invested in an organization and we believe we have a trust to uphold, then we are committed. When we sign a contract, we are committed to fulfill the terms of that contract. That is a transactional commitment, about as far as some employees will go in their commitment to the workplace. Being bound emotionally and intellectually is a step higher on the ladder of commitment. How do we get this level of commitment from those who seem to be satisfied as well as those who are driven by reward systems, personal career me-isms, and the pettiness and envy of everyday work-life? In this age of organizations that are tentative about their commitments, why should we expect something different from employees? The truth is: We are already halfway there but don't know it. We do have a commitment of sorts to our organizations. You have a commitment to yours; I have a commitment to mine. Often, we are emotionally and intellectually bound but do not want to be.

Part of our problem is living in a society that glorifies achievement, comparison, and tentative, partial commitments. In our culture, the grass is viewed as always greener somewhere else. This way of thinking, more than lousy families or incompetent managers, is the reason why people complain so much about their lot in life. People want you to believe that they are the victims of circumstances, that with all their physical, mental, and emotional problems, a government who doesn't care, etc., they had no choice in their situation. If their lot is lousy, it is not because of the decisions they have made. In encapsulated form, just this is the essence of the garden-variety neuroses we find in all of our organizations:

> I have made a series of choices and, in fact at a conscious level, I am satisfied with none of them. What of the opposite mental illness, narcissism (self-centeredness)? I have always been extremely independent and acted in my own best interests. My career, my life, and my ego are #1. I'm not about to let some manager or organization stand in the way of my march to greatness. They, the other members of the organization, have settled; they are chattel. I do not let any commitments bind me other than those to my own career and myself. In due course, my stature will be apparent to everyone.

All of us have a little garden-variety neurosis and narcissism within us. Otherwise, we would not be human. Too much of either in an organization will be a barrier to binding one's self, emotionally and intellectually, to a course of action.

Commitment is Real

I have found that most people who have long-term employment relationships with organizations, when asked if they intend to stay, say yes. Assume for a moment, that this behavioral intention is commitment (Porter and Steer 1979). Believe that no matter what, even people who work in organizations they complain about are committed, as long as they are fastened on the intention to stay. They may change their minds tomorrow, and that is another issue, but we should not confuse what people tell us about their dissatisfactions with lack of commitment to the organization. Put somewhat differently, children are very committed to the families in which they are raised, even if severely dysfunctional. They want to believe that Mom and Dad are truthful and that the microcosm in which they believe is real and hopeful. Therapists can talk all they want about how "your parents didn't love you," but most adult children are having none of it. On some level, none of us can tolerate believing the unthinkable—that our parents did not love us—and all the psychoanalysis in the world won't change this. The same can be said for people in organizations. No matter how unhappy they might seem, people are more committed to organizations than they think: from top management to the lowest-level employee.

Locked In by Ambivalence

In my experience, people have difficulty with a different problem. The real problem for many people is, having made the decision to stay (no matter what the half-life of that decision) accepting that they have made the decision! This is only an apparent conundrum.

We are committed, but wish we weren't. Somehow, committing one's self to a job or organization isn't sexy:

> Don't all the real powerful people in our society own their own businesses; or aren't they stars, famous writers, or Jack Welch? If we are going to work for a company, shouldn't it be as a high-level manager? Should we be satisfied with anything less? Haven't writers like William Bridges (2004) told us that contract employees are best and what we can expect in this best of all possible worlds we face? Many of the good-paying jobs have already gone away. Isn't the world and global competition showing us that you can't trust employers to look out for your well-being?

> Isn't it better to be almost anything but a poor slob working for an organization that is only waiting to give you the axe? (It's just a matter of time.)

In this scenario, isn't tentativeness and disengagement a rational response?

In twenty-first century capitalist America, we want work lives that inflate our sense of self. Often, work has become our primary source of meaning. We find ourselves projecting our poverty of spirit or soul into organizational microcosms of our consumer society. We work and consume in order to feel good about ourselves. Still it is not enough. We want to be great, and our organizations tell us that this is not a realistic objective. There is only so much room for greatness in any organization, and apparently it is found at the top. Our society reinforces grandiosity through the newest emphasis on continuous messaging and blogging. The message seems clear: No matter what is going on in your head, it matters a lot to someone somewhere in cyberspace. We begin to think that everything we do is important. Yet we arrive at the workplace, and most of us are in for a fall. We find that the world does not revolve around us. Work needs to get done, and not all of it is glamorous; in fact, most of it is not. If we are only worth something because we have mountaintop experiences at work or are widely admired for our expertise and reputation, we are living a balloon existence. These things can change in a minute. Tomorrow we could be out on the street. Even if we stay and are committed, there will be times when we will be relatively disengaged. What if, to submit a little counter-cultural conditioning, it doesn't matter where you are in the pecking order, because everybody works for someone else? CEOs report to Boards of Directors and stockholders, consultants are accountable to their clients, famous movie stars are only as famous as their last few pictures (they work for the fickle public).

Grounded in the Day-to-Day

To summarize: Expecting to be great in one's career may set a person up for failure. Anthropologist Ernest Becker (1973) says that the central driving force of the human personality is the quest for the heroic. We seek meaning in a quest larger than ourselves. You may not feel that you have gotten what you deserve in life, or you may feel that you could do better given a new beginning. Should that be the case, you might be feeling pretty depressed right about now. What if both you and I accepted the fact that where we are right now is where we should be? As adults, we have made a series of commitments and decisions that, for whatever reason, have brought us to this point. Maybe we are earning $7.25 an hour (Federal Minimum Wage, 2016) in a non-unionized factory, or maybe we just got a promotion. Maybe we hate our bosses and love our co-workers. Maybe the world is changing rapidly and we are having trouble staying up-to-date with all the newest technology and innovations in our field. Maybe we just got fired for the fourth time. For the moment, can we merely accept who we are and where we are without wanting to be someone else or someplace else? If our organizations do suffer from malaise, part of the problem is just this: We are so preoccupied with *becoming* (and with its imagined fruits) that we do not know how to be. This one fact has powerful ramifications for our work in organizations. For one thing, it means that people aren't fully present for the work that they do. Like presidential candidates, they are always cheating their present job to engage in career enhancement. We suspect that we are better and more powerful than our current job, so why should we get strung-out trying to do a good job in the here and now, just for its own sake. After all, is not everything just a means to an end? Don't we all have to fulfill our deepest potential? Is it not better to be the best and brightest rather than the worst and dumbest?

What five adjectives could be used to describe you that would shame and embarrass you the most? I will bet that many of you would have dumb on that list or, if not dumb, then average. Curse the people who have popularized statistical thinking and the normal distribution curve. Because while it may have great utility for certain purposes, its greatest bane is that it evokes comparison. We need normal distribution curves, do we not? We need to know how to categorize people; to be sure we have assigned them to the right grade in school or the right market segment; to know whether or not one should go to Harvard or the local community college. We simply must know how to pigeonhole you, because if we did not, what on earth would we do with you?

This is exactly what we do with ourselves. We try to pigeonhole our relationship to our world and to ourselves. We are afraid to know who we are at any given moment, because our biggest fear is that we may be nothing. By running from that nothingness, we lose our some-thing-ness; we are always in transition; we are always thinking about the next degree, or job, or book. Now we have come full circle: to the individual who is committed to his job because he/she has decided to stay, for the moment. If we could get ourselves to acknowledge our flight from the present, who knows how much productive energy might be unleashed to accomplish great things right now?

QUESTIONS FOR SELF-ASSESSMENT

1. List the primary organizations you have joined over the course of your life. What was your level of commitment to each? Rate high, medium, or low.

2. Note where your organizational commitments were most tentative. What impact did that have on your subsequent experience of the organization?

3. If you had fully committed yourself to your job or role, how might that have affected you?

REFERENCES

Becker, E. (1997). *The denial of death*. New York, NY: Free Press Paperbacks.

Bridges, W. (2004). *Transitions: Making sense of life's changes, revised 25th anniversary edition*. Boston, MA: Da Capo Press.

Commitment. (n.d.). In *Merriam-Webster's online collegiate dictionary*. Retrieved from http://www.merriam-webster.com/dictionary/commitment

Festinger, L. (1957). *A theory of cognitive dissonance*. Evanston, IL: Row, Peterson.

Porter, L. W. & Steers, R. M. (2002). *Motivation and work behavior* (7th ed.). New York, NY: McGraw-Hill.

From Hierarchies to Gardens

Assume, for a minute, that organizations are not organized. They do not have a top management. The rules and procedures are merely artistic sketches, open to interpretation, and much more fluid than we would imagine them to be. Assume the word "organization" is a linguistic construct whose meaning is relevant to a particular culture or state of consciousness. At will, we can throw that meaning into abeyance. What if our organizations are really worlds of buzzing, blooming confusion, similar to what newborns perceive in the first year after birth (James 1918)? There is a structure of sorts, but it is a deceptive structure. If you had the right eyes to see, you would see that what people in organizations call structure is simply a more or less arbitrary, time-tested pattern that is imposed on human relationships in the way we put a saddle on a horse. It only fits if the horse has already been broken, i.e., has already been subjected to the conditioning existing within the wider society and said yes to that conditioning. Hierarchy, then, will only work for people who have been socialized to hierarchy: have seen it operate in their families of origin, in their schools; have worn the bridle in their mouths and become accustomed to it.

I am talking about you and me. We have all worn the bridle in our mouths; we have all become, more or less, accustomed to it. We tend to focus on top management because we were all children first in family systems that were organized according to principles of rules and hierarchy. In effect, our formative experiences took place in micro-societies where power (buttressed hopefully by love) ruled. We were born into it, trained to follow its rules and logic, and prevented from leaving under pain of survival. It was in this milieu that we first learned about structure, organization, task, and relationship issues.

By the time we have reached the organization for which we will consult or work, we have passed through infinite prisms of conditioning and, if we are lucky, have experienced some novelty and counter-conditioning. We have learned to perceive organizations in a certain way, assume boundaries, compartmentalize our thinking, and at least partially reach a consensus on the work to be done.

Few of us ever question the legitimacy of the cognitive templates that our idiosyncratic brains and society, together, have created and embedded in the structures and processes of our minds. It happened to us automatically as our education/socialization took us from primary process to secondary process thinking, from unconsciousness to consciousness (Freud 1938). We may rebel against parents and convention in the wake of pulsing hormones, but often as not, this rebellion takes place on the unconscious foundation of our earliest conditioning. Society has already made itself at home in our minds. We rebel against the strictures of excessive socialization. In effect, we are the enemy!

An Alternative Reality

Now, from this vantage point, imagine that the word "organization" has been eradicated from the English language and that, instead, we use the term "blossom" to describe the constellations of patterns and processes that we had once subsumed under organization. We do not try to consciously eliminate the linguistic/conceptual debris that has grown up around our old mental models of organization. Instead, we simply apply the logic of blossoming, flowers, and plant life to the reality we thought we always knew. In this world, hierarchy becomes petals, rules become stems, and top management becomes roots. While there is not a one-on-one correspondence with the old language, it is possible for us to appreciate the blossom in ways that it was difficult for us to appreciate the organization. The blossom, for one thing, smells better; we are drawn to it. The blossom is life in the raw without intruding human conventions. Translate our new model into a verb, and there is the implication of new life budding, waiting for just the right combination of moisture and sunlight before erupting into glorious reds or blues. We are blossoms. We consult to blossoms. We work for blossoms, and the world is one big blossom. Consider this: Organizations are just as much blossoms as they are structures, systems, and management practices. The word "organization" has been created by pre-linguistic convention, i.e., out of the chaos of arbitrariness. If we would summon up the courage, we might be willing to boldly see and assert the blossom as a real alternative to conventional reality.

The Executive Gardener

To carry this just a bit further, if organizations were blossoms, as a manager or consultant, I might look to work with those people who had the most potential for growth. They are the budding new models who need a new weather pattern (a new climate) to help them grow. Rather than waste too much time on the dead trees in the organization, I would spread my gardening mix of management practices in the area where the blossoms are most likely to flower. Conversely, I would not assume that all non-performers are lost and without hope; maybe they were simply unaware of what it took to make them grow. Perhaps they were asleep or in a state of dormancy, awaiting an unusual spring for the right conditions to unfold and reveal that mix of sun, moisture, and carbon dioxide that they will need to burst forth from their brownish, weathered shells.

If organizations were blossoms, employees might lose their fear of color and intuition as a basis for making decisions. They might decide to go boldly rampaging through fields of tiger lilies rather than hoarsely stuffing their feelings in an attempt to control behavior and demeanor. Peers might look like friendly fauna, and the magic of childhood might once again be introduced into the barren corporate wilderness. Those who appreciate the simplicity and beauty of the flower would not be oppressed by purveyors of expansion and efficiency. We mock this because, in our culture, we believe in metaphors from sports teams and combat. Where we are aroused by competitive instincts, other cultures see harmony and the extended family. What we see creates our reality. When a significant mass of us see something different from direct reports, for example, the numbers and the bottom-line reality begin to be reconstructed for all of us.

Creativity and Your Prejudices

At this point, the perceptive reader might ask: So what? Why would an executive or manager—even an academic for that matter—give a hoot about unconventional metaphors? I have more important things to do, like worry about reducing costs. The competition is merciless, our country is under terrorist attack, and we're still feeling the pinch of the global meltdown! You don't say? What if seeing things in new and unconventional ways is the precursor to innovation? The conventional business press is full of rhetoric about innovation but sometimes implies that creativity, if it is to be at all relevant, must not go too far outside of the box: Let's hold on to our day-to-day worries and concerns while thinking in a wild way for a few minutes. We know we have to innovate in order to survive. Business books, M. B. A. programs, and even the White House tell us this. Yet we are curiously reluctant to do what must be done to get to the point of innovation: We must turn our current thinking on its head. Are we willing to cast aside the moorings of conventional wisdom and thought models? To take on the experiment of living in an alternative thought-world or culture, throw our current assumptions to the wind, and bring what we have learned back to our day-to-day business reality? Can we be challenged by, assimilate, and integrate what is foreign to our current identity? This is more than thinking outside the box. Outside the box has become a well-worn convention, irrelevant to the paradoxes and dilemmas of our age. Instead the box itself must be thrown away if new and truly original thinking is to emerge. This chapter is not an effort to inject new life into the worn-out term "organization," with all its conceptual baggage. The blossom is an alternative description of the phenomenon we have previously labeled organization. It is not the only possible metaphor nor may it even be the best, but it does imagine and assert a new reality. Executives, managers, and all of us must learn to playfully experiment in this way to clean out the conceptual debris in our minds and keep them in shape. Action is important, and as a nation of entrepreneurs, we rightly prize it. Yet action which is not preceded by creative thought may be another name for stupidity.

QUESTIONS FOR SELF-ASSESSMENT

1. Create a metaphor that helps you reframe your organizational experience(s).

2. Apply that metaphor to your organization and yourself.

3. Act from that metaphorical center for at least one day and record your experiences.

REFERENCES

Freud, S. (1938). *Basic writings of Sigmund Freud.* (A. A. Brill, Trans. & Ed.). New York, NY: The Modern Library.

James, W. (2001). *Psychology: The briefer course.* Mineola, NY: Dover Publications.

Impasse and Transformation

In this chapter, I argue that, while turbulent external change may bring forms of chaos and discomfort to individuals and organizations, the true meaning of chaos is internal. We can tolerate an enormous amount of external change if our personal centers and identity are secure. For that to happen, we will have had to be in the habit of risking those centers by doing what is new and uncomfortable, again and again: That means embracing impasse and its role in experiential learning.

Impasse is the learning point where we have to let go of our old ways of thinking, doing, and being to approach a current challenge in a new and fresh way. To deal with turbulent change, we must be prepared for impasse. This means that we personally must change, and not just change, but transform! To transform is not just a buzz phrase. It has a very concrete, down-to-earth meaning. To transform will mean that the external appearance will probably change; the internal structure, substance, form, and condition will change; and the mind and consciousness will change. There will be a complete conversion and metamorphosis (Ackerman and Ackerman-Anderson 2010). We personally can no longer be old wine in new wineskins. To the extent that we are invested in what is familiar and comfortable, we will resist impasse. Managers and employees are adept at looking as if they are transforming without having actually undergone the painful experience of impasse. To get to impasse we must be able to tolerate, even welcome, at least a mild disconfirmation of our current selves. Many of us are not willing to do that. We want to pretend that everything is always going well. As I illustrate in this chapter, the actual experience of impasse is like Humpty Dumpty falling off his wall. We are never quite sure whether all the king's horses will be able to put us back together.

Unfortunately, our everyday models of personal and organizational development do not consider that significant internal change comes from a potent series of transformational events, punctuated more than once by impasse. As managers, we often fail in trying to develop people and organization because we somehow expect it to be easier. We want seminars, books, and speakers to take the place of personal experience. We think conceptual models and charismatic speakers can penetrate the shell of conditioning that holds our deeper identities intact. (As Shakespeare would have it, this is, in fact, "the rub.")

There is much good literature available today on how organizations change and develop and what it takes to catalyze change (see Cummings and Worley 2009). Noted theorists and practitioners agree that today's organizations face white-water conditions (Vaill 1996). It is no longer necessary to unfreeze (Lewin and Gold 1999) organization and human behavior patterns in order to kick-start change. Alternatively, we don't need complex theories to tell us that conditions are chaotic. I wonder if our experience of chaos in organizations and society is as much a reflection of internal instability as it is of external change. Looking back over our history, we can see many periods in this country where people lived with high levels of change and uncertainty: Time periods surrounding the Revolution, the Declaration of Independence, the Civil War, the Great Depression, World War II, and the Civil Rights Movement. Through all these events, the center arguably held.

Chaos, Complexity, and Order

It is useful to make a conceptual bridge between chaos and complexity theories to illustrate that as a society of organizations, we are not without moorings, and that chaos is, at least partially, a phenomenon of perceptual set (Butz 1997). Chaos theory was borrowed from the natural sciences and physics, and then applied to psychology and organizational change phenomena. As originally contrived, it was not only about instability and turbulence. The intention was that chaos be viewed within the context of systems thinking and phased periods of dynamic systems evolution. These phases are entitled: (1) Change; (2) Chaos; (3) Complexity (Butz 1997). A second book on chaos theory reinforces the validity of such thinking (Kellert 1993). Briefly, the author states that chaotic phenomena are not without patterns. If we only knew enough about the conditions that created the chaos—i.e., earlier stages of system evolution, as well as other forces operating within the system—we might be in a better position to see both order and turbulence. Consider, for example, the recent economic meltdown. It was global. The changes in global political and economic systems leading up to it had been mounting incrementally for decades (Cooper 2008). The situation had begun to descend into chaos earlier than the fall of 2008. The chaotic phase itself stretched back at least a year. The media and the public were simply not focusing on this larger picture until momentum accelerated and there was an eruption into devastating and chaotic results: Housing mortgages became toxic, and major U.S. companies began entering into federal receivership. The center seemed to be giving way, and metaphors such as approaching the edge of the cliff were tossed around left and right. This might only have been a half-truth. Within the chaotic phase, during its upside, global leaders began experimenting with many unconventional ideas, such as temporary federal government ownership of private businesses. Communication gaps were bridged and new levels of global cooperation quickly evolved. One could argue that the global political and economic system is already evolving into a new level of order and complexity. This is the third phase of system evolution. We don't know what it will ultimately look like, or even if it is sustainable, but *The Economist* (2016) at least sometimes feels comfortable risking the perception that the worst is behind us. (This may change tomorrow, if terrorism continues its pandemic reach or the Eurozone plunges into economic chaos, but cautious optimism is the current way of things.) Our world and its economic and political systems may still look chaotic, but they are full of patterns and always tending toward the establishment of new ones. As organizations and individuals face the turbulence, we often fail to see the patterns.

Our fear of chaos has less to do with the absence of order than with our fear that we will be pushed beyond our limits, forced to give up that which makes us comfortable, and driven to stand alone over our own inner abyss. (Consider this a hypothesis and then think it through for yourself.) This abyss is the place where our sense of identity and inner continuity break down in the face of external shocks and disruptions. For example, our sense of "I" becomes more fluid and dynamic as we go through a merger or downsizing. What was a coherent and structured self has a tendency to become fragmented, weakened, and full of frailties. We feel differently, and we see ourselves differently. External change forces us to embrace new adaptations. To embrace change, we have to let go of the coherent "I" we have created over the years. If we realize we are unfit for the new and difficult challenges we face—and many do not—we may seek to change ourselves to meet that new reality. To the extent that we lack a center and have not significantly risked our identities before, this experience can be daunting. For those who have conspired in allowing external factors to define them (employment relationships, families, church memberships, or business associations) it will probably mean higher levels of fear and uncertainty. Letting go to experience the personal center, the core personality beyond all roles, may mean a descent through layers of ignored reality. We experience pain, fear, depression, and anger as repressed parts of our personality are born in the midst of an internal destruction and cleansing of an incomplete, role-bound self. We are not the persons we thought we were. Adversity is beginning to reveal both the character flaws and strengths of the real person.

Facing the Real Inner Man (Generic)

This is a time of great opportunity for any of us to become larger than what we were, to become whole and more complete people. In fact, the building up of the center comes from having faced this abyss, or what is incomplete in our lives, again and again over the course of a lifetime. Even for those who have significantly risked themselves before, the pain of facing inner chaos is daunting. To do so is to risk psychological death: the possibility that when Humpty Dumpty begins to break down in the face of complex external demands, it may not be possible for the people we previously were to put Humpty back together. If we try to smooth it over and go back to the way we were, we may end up looking the same to others. However, we will often find over time that a part of us has calcified. If we pull back from what externally defines us to turn inward and face who we really are without the masks and social defenses, we face either inadequacy and dissolution or the opportunity for dynamic growth and personal completion. This is a real impasse, a choice with no easy way out. Herein lies the real chaos: Will we go forward or backward? Will we choose psychological life or death? Where will we end up? That is what happens when external structures like organizations break up in events like downsizing or meltdown, and the individual is left alone, comparatively naked, to face himself.

Impasse: The Great Liberator

The issue of change and the inner self is an important one because it is connected to the role of impasse as an organizational metaphor. When asked, How should we prepare our organizations for the challenges of the twenty-first century? our answer should be, Prepare them, and yourselves, for impasse. After that, and comparatively speaking, we can relax, because there is no step-by-step way to prepare. Over time, as we attempt to adapt to external change, we will be gripped by impasse in the normal course of things. Having tried all of the ways we know to respond to external change, having run the gamut of doing more with less or how to reengineer our workplace in ten easy steps, we discover that it will not work to package old wine in new wineskins. Change Programs will no longer do it for us:

> I will step-out on a limb and confess. I have sometimes tried to apply linear models of personal and professional development to my life. At times I would have been happier if everything had always been under my tight control. I wanted to get ahead

and do it my way. This would mean less vulnerability and lower risk for me. Many other times I have opted for adventure and less control. I became more vulnerable in the process, but the potential rewards were greater. I learned more, and I changed. I improved. I matured. The key in my case was a change of character. I was willing to give up an old self to be become a new and improved version. I could not predict that it would turn out that way, but I took a risk. When the challenges of life demand that we change if we want to live a full and complete life, we had better listen. These challenges are almost always asking for some form of personal transformation. The other options are less inviting: Self-protection, smallness, retreat, and/or retirement. Some people will choose one of these options, and for them it is a deliberate, conscious choice. Temporarily, it might not be a bad choice. Many others will unconsciously slip into one of these. That is a tragedy. For the long haul, if you want to remain vital in your life, work, and career, these other choices won't work.

For many organizations, the management of change often consists of responding to external change without first changing ourselves internally, and from the inside out. (Change practitioners are familiar with this phenomenon of pretending to change while psychologically and behaviorally reaffirming the old work identity and role behaviors.)

To continue this undesirable scenario: As a manager, I may have more problems. Chances are, as uncertainty goes up for the organization (and me) I might try to shove your square employee peg into an organizational round hole. Then I will deny the meanness and irrationality of what I have done. It is easier for me to force-fit old concepts and methods than it is for me to stand with a certain amount of fear and trembling and face the fact that I don't know what to think or do. The more rapidly things may be changing around me, the less adequate I may feel and the more often I may not know what to do. Unfortunately, managers are paid to know what to do, the buck has to stop somewhere, and you better not show weakness if you plan to get ahead around here. Let's deny our inadequacies and force-fit our strengths! It is less messy that way and more manly, both for men and women.

People, managers, and organizations all resist impasse: We want to be in control as we learn! That, of course, is an oxymoron. There is plenty of evidence in life, and in psychotherapist's offices, that impasse is the great teacher. When you have tried everything you can think of to resolve a problem, situation, or dilemma, when there is no easy way to exit the field, and the forces for change are continuing to build, how do you feel? If you are normal, you may feel helpless, frustrated, scared, and even enraged. How do you act? If you are a manager, you may try to cover up your feelings and act normally. Over time, this is a fruitless endeavor. More than likely, such efforts will be punctuated by periods of venting or acting out where you take out your feelings of being thwarted on your immediate neighbors. It helps if they have less power. (Of course, this may not fit for everyone. You and your colleagues may have it all together with outlets for these kinds of tensions. Things change, however, and impasses have a way of deepening.) The most painful impasse is the one where your slack or wiggle room is severely constricted. An addict of the new and novel, your organization may have tried every management fad there is from *10 Steps to Quick*

Transformation to *Downsizing for Dummies*. Fads have a way of fooling everyone into thinking they are doing something meaningful. This is an example of activity reducing anxiety and driving out learning. However, impasse occurs when you are really at loggerheads and fads leave you cold. Impasse exists when things in the organization are approaching the point of being out of control, or you fear losing control and the fixes come quicker and quicker with a descending gradient of effectiveness. (Managers and executives, please do not be offended. I am not saying you are not mature, competent, and capable. I am talking about systemic challenges that face all of us when major adversity hits our workplace. I am saying adversity will reveal character. I am not saying that character cannot be changed! It also depends on the individual, their level of consciousness and motivation.)

Impasse is Like Dying Unless You Are Fully Alive!

Impasse is a descent into the nature of things, a willingness to temporarily fall apart in the face of forces that call the very structure of your character into question. Impasse is French existential philosopher Jean Paul Sartre's *No Exit* (1958), a coming to terms with the best and the worst in you. It is very simply letting go of what you already know, cognitively and consciously, to trust in the emergent knowledge that can now come only from the subconscious and unconscious processes within yourself. That's right: The knowledge that is going to help you cope or save your job needs to bubble up creatively from somewhere inside you which you cannot totally control. What's more, if you have the wrong kind of character structure, and your control needs are high, it's probably going to hurt when this new baby is born. Managers are paid to control things, to reduce uncertainty, to produce. However, when the ground shifts, they, like everyone else, are confronted by the unworn and untested within themselves, comparatively naked before the forces of dislocation and implicitly afraid of impasse.

Up Against It: A Case Example

Let us take an example to illustrate the arguments I have made in this chapter: As a change consultant in California, I worked extensively with transit organizations. The typical transit agency is public, non-profit, and structured to ensure safe, efficient transportation services, on time, at a reasonable cost. In a mundane sense, this means layers of rules and regulations, structures and scheduling processes built on a rational model of organizing. It may also mean alienated, disaffected coach operators. First-line supervisors are frequently a fragmented group. Operators have infrequent communications with a rotating group of individual supervisors over a period of weeks or months. Coach operators are out on the road by themselves most of the time, and when necessary, they contact a supervisor who is available, not necessarily the one to whom they are assigned. It is a "catch as catch can" kind of supervision: Few formal meetings, very little time for coaching or mentoring, and coach operators who are most closely connected to their organization through their union steward. The tie to the larger organization is minimal. Conversely, and to their credit, operators believe in their ability to serve their customers and in the integrity of their agency and its organizational identity, at least symbolically. The organizational identity is what is central to the transit organization both as real organization and as symbolic entity (Hatch and Schulz 2010). The concept organizational identity means, and implicitly poses the question: Who are we, beyond the structures, practices, systems, and processes, all of which can and ought to change as external factors shift? Who are we in our organizational core beyond the epiphenomenon of organization? Knowing who we are, as well as what business we are in, is central to maintaining a coherent identity in the midst of turbulent global change. If we do not know who we are and why we exist, we are easy prey for other organizations and privatized competitors who do. The organizing problem which accompanies the concept of organizational identity is: How do we distinguish between what is central and what is peripheral to our organizational identity? How do we build an infrastructure to support what is central?

The Organization on the Couch

The developmental psychoanalyst Erik Erickson says that individual identity is formed through the interaction of individual egos and the collectivity of egos, in the wider sphere of social interaction, over time (2001). If we apply a related set of concepts to transit organizations, then as the external environment goes into dynamic overdrive, the organization must learn to stay in touch with what is central to itself, while continuing to connect with the elements of its environment that are central to its ongoing existence. Linking to customers, funding agencies, private sector partners, and all levels of government, is critical; but to survive, grow, and prosper, the organization must also remain true to what is central in itself. To maintain or reconnect with its core identity, the agency, like the individual, must turn inward toward its values. It has to surface, re-examine, and reformulate them in the light of current reality. What is dysfunctional must be thrown aside; what is essential must be welded to and must drive its current mission and strategy. Without confronting itself and its readiness for real change, the organization will play-act at change. Just when the stakes are highest, when its future is at stake, the agency will embrace fads and programs. Like individuals, it is running from impasse. It does not want to experience the pain that inevitably accompanies rediscovery of the true organizational self. While an organization can plan for the future and hope to apply rational, orderly methods to its day-to-day activity, discovering who it is, at a gut-level, means to face impasse that pushes beyond the superficial organizing tools and structures.

Getting Through the Eye of the Needle

Having explored the phenomenon of impasse, how do we get to and through it to find a solution to the agency's real problems of existence? How do we make the agency robust and suitable for a complex evolving world? No outsider, no matter how expert, has the solution to the problems of the organization and its future. The best thing a consultant can do it to suggest questions that agency leaders might ask themselves. Since we cannot change without first knowing who we are, a particular agency might need to ask the paradoxical question: Is an alienated community of coach operators central to our identity? Is it something like culture that is assimilated at a bone-deep level and that is intractable, maybe impossible to change? This is not an idle question. Transit organizations act as if it were so. They do not experiment with changes that would threaten the core alienation of operators. What leads them to change, at this level, if they are even able to do so, is the realization that the current identity, which includes alienated operators, may not be compatible with survival. Transit organizations come to this realization irrationally.

For example, given the problem of deteriorating coach operator attitudes toward customers, the organization will focus on: (1) Tightening up discipline; (2) Customer relations training; (3) Leadership development; and finally, if they are really courageous, (4) Changing the culture, management practices, and assumptions of the workplace for optimal customer focus and employee community. Only the gutsy ones will finally do number four, because it is a process which requires participants to experience the fear and inadequacy of impasse. The first three are useful things to do, no question, but to be successful they will need to tap core values and beliefs in the operators and supervisors themselves. As long as operators believe that most supervisors are confused, powerless, or incompetent, no force-feeding of concepts and skills is going to convince them otherwise. To develop in this respect, operators will need to think through and enact their whole gamut of conditioned responses and beliefs. They will need to feel safe while doing so. They must interact with supervisors who are open, tough, and supportive. It may be necessary to fight with managers who refuse to be pigeonholed. Then they may be able to reach their own personal impasse and let go of long-standing prejudices and stereotypes about management. They cannot be controlled into relinquishing their self-protective shells to embrace a rational concept like "we [the company] are the team." They cannot be bullied with rhetoric, however well-meaning and benevolent sounding, and they cannot be conditioned with new skills training and concepts. For any person to change, a willingness and openness is needed—a desire to see things differently! That only comes from individuals and groups facing and interacting with each other long enough and intensely enough to see what each is made of: What is central and what is peripheral. Normally, this will mean holding on to their defensive postures and experiential programming until face-to-face with impasse. A summary of the stages and accompanying mindsets and behavior is presented below:

Out the Other Side

Phases	Mindset and Behaviors
1. The ground for new learning	A willingness and desire to see things differently
2. Letting down your guard	I could be wrong, taking risks by discussing the previously un-discussable
3. The freshness of open communication	Accepting both early success and failure
4. Shattering the stereotypes	More experimentation and efforts to connect at the level of feelings; tolerance for expression of negative feelings
5. New models, training, experiences, time, and gradual willingness to let go of personal defenses	Boldness, desire for engagement, connecting behaviors, organizational reinforcement

Put differently, I will resist seeing you as you are until you let down your guard to show me more of what is real in you. You will resist seeing me differently until I change some of my basic attitudes and behaviors and enact the new possibilities in your presence. And neither of us is likely to see or act differently unless we're pushed up against the wall, confronted by the limitations of our own previous thinking and experiences. I have to see that I was wrong about you and about myself. You're smarter than I thought; you can get angry and take charge. All these years I have been making excuses for myself and my part in this organizational play by blaming it all on you. Both of us have hidden behind the protection afforded by the hardened roles and stereotypes of the reality that we have collectively created. I'm not likely to become a better coach, and you're not likely to be a better operator, until we've both hit the wall and felt the limitations of this limited way of being. We need to do this until it is no longer possible for us to go on as before. New models, new training, new experiences, time, and gradual willingness to let go of our defenses, to unlearn and re-learn, are all essential. They will not be successful unless they lead us into and through the experience of impasse. On Saturday Night Live, comedian Jon Lovitz used to joke about, yet embrace, solutions to his problems that came very cheaply: "Yeah, that's the ticket!" (Downey and Chase 1985). Just so, there is a ticket here, and yet it is quite expensive. If we are to change, we will need to find a way to accelerate learning to the point of impasse. The irony is, this will not happen by dumping a lot of new responsibilities on people, or training them to death, or forcing them to work seventy-hour weeks. These things are likely to harden defenses and prevent any learning from occurring. Put another way, the marketing, speed mentality alone will not do the job!

QUESTIONS FOR SELF-ASSESSMENT

1. Think of an example when you experienced impasse as part of your work. Describe that experience along with the feelings and behaviors that accompanied it.

2. Explain how impasse might have motivated you to see, think, or do things differently in the situation.

3. Look at the core identity of an organization with which you are associated. Describe it in one sentence or less, and ask yourself what the organization could jettison or change while still retaining its core identity. (Your answer is probably what it should change.)

REFERENCES

Blanchard, K. H. & Johnson, S. (1982). *The one-minute manager*. New York, NY: William Morrow.

Butz, M. R. (1997). *Chaos and complexity*. Washington, D.C.: Taylor & Francis.

Carroll, L. (2010). *Alice in wonderland*. New York, NY: Tribeca Books.

Cooper, G. (2008). *The origins of financial crises: Central banks, credit bubbles, and the efficient market fallacy*. New York, NY: Vintage Press.

Cummings, T. G., & Worley, C. G. (2009). *Organizational development and change*. Mason, OH: Southwestern Cengage Learning.

Downey, J. (Head writer) & Chase, C. (Host). (1985). Pathological liars anonymous [Television series episode] in *SNL Transcripts*, Session 11, Episode 2. Retrieved from http://snltranscripts.jt.org/85/85bliar.phtml

Erikson, E. & Coles, R. (2001). *The Erik Erikson reader*. New York, NY: W. W. Norton.

Hammer, M. & Champy, J. (2003). *Reengineering the corporation: A manifesto for business revolution*. New York, NY: Harper.

Hatch, M. J. & Schultz, M. (2004). *Organizational identity: A reader*. Oxford, GB: Oxford University Press.

Kellert, S. H. (1993). *In the wake of chaos: Unpredictable order in dynamical systems*. Chicago, IL: University of Chicago Press.

Lewin, K. & Gold, M. (ed.). (1999). *The complete social scientist: A Kurt Lewin reader*. Washington, D. C.: American Psychological Association Publications.

Impasse (n. d.). *Merriam-Webster's online collegiate dictionary*. Springfield, MA: Merriam-Webster. Retrieved from http://www.merriam-webster.com/dictionary/impasse

Sartre, J. (1958). *No exit & three other plays*. New York, NY: Vintage Books.

Shakespeare, W. To be or not to be. In *Wickipedia* (April 20, 2012). Retrieved from http://en.wikipedia.org/wiki/To_be_or_not_to_be_(Shakespeare)

Vaill, P. B. (1996). *Learning as a way of being: Strategies for survival in a world of permanent white water*. San Francisco, CA: Josey-Bass.

PSYCHOLOGICAL DILEMMAS OF LEADERSHIP

Each year hundreds of books and thousands of articles are written on the topic of leadership. It seems that in our time, we cannot get enough of leadership frameworks and models. One might well ask, Why all the fuss? Surely many of us have grown up with at least a few role models and, as we matured, stepped up to the mantle of leadership. We have probably done this a number of times. Why is it today that we seem to need so much guidance and handholding? (That we do, I think, is inarguable.) The billions spent on books, seminars, and training make the point very effectively. Is it because the forces of global change render most of our leadership skills obsolete? Are we forced to keep cramming just to stay in place? With so much knowledge and leadership development occurring, why is there is still so much angst about leadership? Eichinger and Lombardo (2007) have done extensive research over several decades and have discovered sixty-seven different leadership competencies. They claim that there is now enough sophisticated knowledge available to develop all of our executives and managers into leaders, if they are willing to make the commitment. These are distinguished experts—leaders in their field—and they are saying we know enough to get the job done. Yet we continue to search for something more. I think what we are looking for has less to do with skills, competencies, and development and more to do with who we are as people. In this essay, I want to explore the idea that it is the natural subjectivity of the leader, the ways in which each leader marshals the contradictions within themselves, that constitutes the heart of leadership.

Leadership Through the Ages

Theories of leadership stretch back into time. They are both explicit and implicit in sacred texts like the Bible. More recently, in the social scientific tradition, Burns has published the definitive tome on the topic (1978). There is much to be admired in recent books and journals on leadership, but it is not my purpose to investigate that literature. Instead, I intend to restore a phenomenological element to leadership theory and look at leadership dilemmas from the point of view of the individual actor in his situation. Classics of literature are more appropriate for such a job. Great writers are adept at bringing personal contradictions and dilemmas to the forefront. What we may lose in analytical precision, we gain in insight and understanding.

Purpose in the Face of the Storm

Homer's *Odyssey* is a prime example (2006). The story begins at the end of the Trojan Wars when Odysseus, a Greek leader of will and purpose, begins the long journey home to his wife and family. During the voyage, he undergoes many trials as a variety of gods, physical dangers, and natural disasters threaten to defeat his mission. Ultimately, it takes him ten years to reach Ithaca, his homeland, and he arrives only to discover that traitors are threatening his throne. Acting stealthily, he disguises himself, gains entry to his palace, and overcomes his enemies. There is much more to this epic saga, but the lesson seems clear: One essential of leadership is dogged pursuit of purpose while facing high and sustained levels of uncertainty. Much like Odysseus had to contend with sirens, Cyclops, and the unpredictability of the gods, modern day leaders of organizations must persist in going beyond the limits of the business universe as they have known it.

Groundhog Day

Franz Kafka, in his great novel, *The Trial* (1999), shows how individual autonomy and leadership potential can be stymied by a combination of personal weakness, breakdowns in society, and social control. Joseph K., a common man, wakes up one day, accused of a crime he knows he did not commit. He is kept from learning anything about the charges but must report to court on a regular basis. As in the movie, Groundhog Day (1993), every day is a recurring dream. It never stops. In the end, he begins to feel crazy, as nothing ever gets resolved. Life goes on, and he becomes more and more uncertain of his fate. His ability to work and sustain personal relationships sours. The more he tries to gain control, the more hopeless his situation becomes. Though apparently unrelated to modern leadership issues, this story illustrates the impossibility of individual empowerment and high performance without change to the social and organizational forces that hinder autonomy and initiative. Although few of us live in a totalitarian state like the one experienced by Joseph K., organizations do generate forces that hinder individual and team enterprise. The larger and more bureaucratic the organization, the more likely this is to happen. Ultimately, it is the responsibility of organizational leaders to see that employees are empowered and held accountable, that external forces do not intrude upon the organization's values and integrity, and that necessary rules, policies, and procedures do not become ends in themselves.

Man and Superman

In *Thus Spake Zarathustra*, Friedrich Nietzsche's brilliant philosophical masterpiece, the central character is an individual who believes he has ascended to the level of human development where human beings belong (Kauffmann 1995). Zarathustra is the symbol of a superior and evolved sort of man, propounding philosophical and religious challenges to a society of herd creatures (presumably, the rest of us). In fact, Zarathustra is the author's mouthpiece; he is Nietzsche. In a general sense, Nietzsche has compassion for his fellow man. However, he cannot help but scorn man's willingness to abrogate personal freedom and responsibility. In truth, he wants all of humanity to join him in the noble isolation of transcendent leadership, to realize that man and only man is responsible for his destiny. Leaders in our modern organizations ought to take his message to heart. If leaders would rise above the circumstances of their individual roles, they would know that they bear responsibility for all that happens in their organizations, even if they are not directly involved. As leaders, we must plead mea culpa. We cannot blame circumstances or others.

In each of these examples, the protagonist-leader is everyman. Taken together, these profound works get at the full range of human emotions and the combination of personal strength and weakness in the human personality. They imply that leadership power, as often as not, comes from the inside out and depends less on context and situational factors than we might be led to think. Even Kafka's Joseph K. has the power to choose his thoughts and behaviors, although his whole environment seems to be going mad. When creative artists write about leadership, it is often within a veiled context. Leadership emerges through a series of dilemmas that the potential leaders wrestle with. The outcome is by no means certain. Personal weakness and foibles are frequently shown to be at the very heart of the matter. The would-be leader is thrown into a particular world without any certain knowledge of what is expected of him or her. What is certain is that there are a series of situations present, and the actor is required to make sense of them and respond in some manner. For Nietzsche, the final result of this situation is the opportunity for man to overcome his baser nature. In his philosophy, one sees the existential struggles that finally culminate in the loneliness and isolation which often accompany transcendence of self. Yet from that very perch of loneliness, he still attempts to lead and to call his fellow human beings to a higher standard.

Nietzsche's philosphy has pragmatic ramifications which apply for all time. There is a price to be paid by those who would lead. The greater or more radical the leadership, the greater the price. The comforts of conformity with the group, the body politic, or the state are lost forever. This is a flesh and blood leadership that is earned; not so much the Great Man Theory as the Fallible Men and Women Theory. Begin with a bundle of personal contradictions; imagine an individual suffering in the throes of these contradictions. Believe, like Kierkegaard (1999) that to lead from that individual center is to lead with fear and trembling, no guarantees.

Leading From the Personal Center

The reality of leaders both strong and weak contrasts markedly with the charismatic theory of leadership, at least the way we often understand it. Popular culture would have us believe that charisma is a special magic that only a few have. Tough luck, in this age of change, if you do not have it. This author sees it differently: The magnetism and charm exuded by the charismatic personality is very much a combination of the dynamic interplay of strength, weakness, and inner complexity. We, the leader in us, gives off excitement as we struggle to overcome our flaws and to come to terms with who we are at any given moment in time. We may disbelieve our own charisma—we all have some— because we are still full of the culturally shared images of the great man.

We are all too ready to believe in the Wizard of Oz leadership theory (Fleming and LeRoy 1939). In this very wise children's fantasy, the Wizard is a powerful symbol of God, good parents, and coming home to one's self. We, along with Dorothy, Tin Man, Scarecrow, and the Lion are seduced into believing the charismatic emperor-leader can make the lost and incomplete whole. If we close our eyes and believe—"there's no place like home"—we may yet end up back in Kansas under the protection of the wise and all-powerful Auntie Em. In reality, back in the workplace, whenever we look for leaders who will promise us paradise or make us feel secure, we are sacrificing our freedom to a tin god, whether they actually appear on the stage or not.

In the final moments of the film, the wizard's charisma is shown to be false. We can see that his is the unexamined life, a posturing affectation. Behind the bravado is a timid soul. Paradoxically, he only becomes genuine when he drops the mask and becomes honest about who he is, a normal human being. Only then can weakness (in his case, genuine regret, feeling, and compassion; the very emotions that were denied by The Wizard persona) transform into something higher.

The popular appetite for what I am calling false charisma is a bad habit; it causes individuals in organizations to feel less powerful themselves. Leadership should be seen as something other than a fixed commodity reserved for those who are ambitious and driven. In reality, it is often those who can tolerate and confront both internal conflict and self-doubt who will come away prepared for organizational leadership in an age of complexity. Drive and ambition are only constructs, often self-descriptions that we present to the world. The internal situation may be much more complex.

Leaders evolve as they return to the focal conflicts and themes of internal ambivalence that represent points of strength and weakness for them. These, like dependence and rebellion, pugnacity or passivity, have their roots in the distant past. The external world chides and demands, and leadership is evoked as individuals face their own personal abyss. That abyss is the gap between what is time-worn and tested in a person and what remains to be grasped in the spontaneity of the moment. It is the individual reaching beyond his traits of character. Circumstance and individual projects combine to evoke existential questions that must be answered at key transition points in life and work: Who am I? What do I stand for? What shall I do? These questions are not tied to any one organization or setting but have ramifications for all of the settings in which we intend to exercise our leadership. Leadership is only one of many possible responses to this eternal sequence of dilemmas. Many of us would prefer to deny the questions and therefore end up on automatic, squandering our powers in false consciousness and self-delusion (Sartre 1956).

Risk, Action, and Organizational Complexity

Coping with complexity in one's organizations and in society depends on one's ability to risk one's self. The one sure road to failure is to tire of facing the unknown and withdraw to a comfortable mental schoolroom where yesterday's answers to today's problems are taught. Alternatively, risking one's self is no guarantee of personal or organizational success. The risk takers will surely be wrong from time to time, maybe often. The central thing executive action does do is reframe the context for everyone. For example, if I as manager have admitted I do not have all the answers, and yet I am still willing to try something new in the face of unique challenges, I am saying to all constituencies that they too must commit to courageous action. You cannot ask me to lead and execute while you cling to the past. I am demonstrating to you that stepping out on faith is the essence of all leadership. If you demand, however, that the element of risk be minimized in favor of tried and true solutions, you are misreading the situation. If tried and true solutions really worked most of the time in this age of discontinuity, then most of our organizations would have reached the Golden Age. Many organizations are really good at reinventing the obvious under a new name. When faced with a true social innovation like transformational leadership (Burns 1995), the average organization will try to re-conceptualize and repackage the phrase in order to fit it more effectively into the current outmoded frame. Instead of seeing the revolutionary implications of this innovation for increased organizational effectiveness, they will try to extract the promised silver bullet, tear it from its context and graft it onto an organizational milieu that does not fully understand either transformation or leadership. The executives in such an organization are demonstrating the mechanistic-control model of organizations. They are substituting enthusiasm and rhetoric for true change. Even the old Communists in the now defunct USSR were great at sloganeering and creating the posture of effective leadership while securing greater and greater control. The situation may be getting better as we all learn how to face the realities of constant change, but it has not gone away.

Leader as Learner

An effective leader is, first of all, a learner who is able to step outside the shared assumptive base of the organization, and, like a child, ask, Why does this happen? Why are we doing this? Who benefits from this practice? Leaders are able to partially detach from a matrix within which they have a major investment and think about it from a counter-cultural point of view. Leaders will not embrace novelty for its own sake. Having thought deeply about their own organization and its need to change (or not), they will also think deeply about what medicine the organization needs to take to get healthy. To stay with our example, a learner, when faced with the question, Should we create a culture of transformational leadership? might ask, What is the reality behind transformational leadership? The phrase is a stepchild of management gurus and book fly leafs. What, in fact, does it mean to lead transformation-ally? What kind of organization should or would want to be transformed? What do you really gain by transforming management, employees, or the work itself? Who benefits? Who loses? Are there any sustained benefits for the team, organization, and customer, or is it a phrase that symbolizes our tendency to want something for nothing (minimal investment equals minimal outcome)? A leader is always ready to question what is popular or current rather than posing naive questions that unveil the emperor without his clothes. In today's media and information soaked world, where the sheer quantity of data lulls us to sleep, it is not easy to apply the rules of critical thinking to the executive function in each of us.

When Weakness and Strength Collide

A leader frequently derives strength from adversity. However, the causal sequence that produces the result may be anything but linear. Winston Churchill, for example, is often presented as a paragon of leadership virtue (Gilbert 1995). He is seen as strong and single-minded. Yet for many years of his political life, his career progress was up-and-down. Over the course of his life he suffered from depression and alcohol abuse. While he achieved career success early, he also lost it a number of times. Looked at a bit one-sidedly, he was at risk for failing to reach his full potential. Conversely, if one reviews the spectacular accomplishments of his later years, one can see that he overcame the negative odds in his life to successfully lead England in its fight against Nazism. In fact, he was most successful when the adversity was greatest! When Hitler had crushed France, and the British Army was hobbling toward the evacuation at Dunkirk, Churchill was reviewing the situation in the field and experiencing a realistic sense of foreboding and despair (1991). He was a man familiar with depression and one who had fought recurrent feelings of hopelessness all his life. What he brought with him to this poignant moment was the experience of successfully overcoming his condition again and again. More than once, he had risen from his own personal pit to reaffirm a positive identity. This very background superbly equipped him to lead his country out of the depths and despair of World War II. Unlike men or women who may have suffered less, he knew too well that no matter how bleak things looked, no matter how bad we may feel, there is ultimate hope and inspiration in believing there is a way out. He knew from experience that you won't always see the specifics of the hoped-for path when you first set your jaw. Simply hoping and believing that some sort of success is still possible, simply refusing to ultimately submit to your own low morale is one essential for leadership. It is frequently the overcoming of personal weakness or character flaws that teaches the best lessons about strength and tenacity. Testing one's mettle against these personal demons is far more challenging than any external threats we may face.

Richard Nixon and the Demons of Self-Pity

President Richard Nixon knew this but failed to fully accept the messages and teachings of his own flaws (1962). He was a man haunted by the ghosts of the past. When he failed, as he did a number of times, he frequently refused to acknowledge his own part in the loss. He projected his personal failures onto enemies and then erected an edifice of self-justification to help him tolerate his own lies. As is often true when experience and strength fail to mature into wisdom, Nixon ended up stumbling over his own self-hatred.

Nixon was certainly a man of contradictions and a fighter. Like Churchill, he could do well in adversity. Unlike Churchill, however, he used adversity as an excuse to aggrandize himself in his own eyes, to puff himself up, as it were. Churchill was more aware of and seasoned in his experience of self. He could acknowledge his flaws and somehow own them in a deeper way than Nixon. Paradoxically, it is just this acceptance of that imperfection in the self that enables the leader to rally his equally imperfect followers.

The Gift of Humility

In her developmental model of early childhood, psychoanalyst Melanie Klein discusses the evolution of certain psychological states (1975). She believed these states are, in some sense, determinate for later development and that one could get stuck in their residue. Klein speaks of the paranoid position where children project their imperfections onto others. She also illuminates the depressive position, a cognitive-emotional state characterized by despair and self-blame. Nixon projected his imperfections onto others, the essence of Klein's paranoid position. History tells us that Churchill sometimes wallowed in depressive blackness, Klein's depressive position. According to her model, depression is developmentally more advanced than paranoia, but one might argue that each of the positions constitutes a threat to the development of healthy leadership.

Fortunately, Churchill was able to overcome his psychological baggage though a combination of creativity and wit. Although capable of hatred and blame—ironically, like Hitler, adept at characterizing his enemies as nemeses—unlike Hitler, he did this in a way that was psychologically adaptive, both for himself and for his nation (Waite 1997). If he hated the Nazis and could arouse his people to collective hatred, this had its utility. In addition, from reading his books, one is left with the feeling that his verbal attacks on the common enemy were less than personal. His revered speech, "We will fight them on the beaches…" seems to have had less to do with conquering the enemy than it did with showing leadership to the British people and rallying them from a losing position (Gilbert 1995). One can imagine Sir Winston with a sparkling glint in his eye as he inspires his people to glory, perhaps laughing at his own grandiose rhetoric. Rather than needing to be a hero, he could consciously subordinate himself to the personal style and dominance traits of a Franklin Roosevelt in order to foster a greater good. In modern terms, this is called having humility and grace. The leader who is full of ego is unwilling to do such a thing. These individuals dare not risk their fragile egos by admitting they are anything less than strong and heroic. Hitler was like this, Nixon was like this, and this was the mythic hero of the American West, the cowboy. Ironically, John Wayne, our WWII cowboy war hero seems, in retrospect, to have had less bravado than is ascribed to him. Watching his movies, one can often see his style as ambling and even mildly self-disparaging. He is more of a person with strengths, weaknesses, and a sense of humor. We can forgive our leaders their weaknesses; we often do. We can never forgive them their mean-spiritedness and self-importance.

Backing Away from Leadership

In organizations, leaders sometimes lack the flexibility to roll with the punches. For those still conditioned to the comforts and order of hierarchy, there is an ever-present danger that the messiness of change will undermine their sense of who they are and the status and prerogatives that go with that role identity. There is always the temptation to preserve islands of certainty in the sea of change. Of course, there is nothing wrong with wanting structure, some direction and focus to guide action. When you are trying to implement change, this may even be more important. However, when leaders begin looking for new forms of bureaucracy to buffer themselves from the demands of leadership or distance themselves from their employees, you can be sure that personal growth and organizational transformation are not priorities.

In my consulting work, the one thing I understood early on was this: Our ability to help organizations change in a deep way depends on our ability to help formal leaders change themselves. If they are not up to it, we should help them consciously opt out of the formal leadership role. Leadership transformation requires a great deal of individual self-awareness and the willingness to be disconfirmed, both by self and others in the organization. Stepping away from the leadership of change is difficult; in practice it often fails to happen. Senior executives may hold on to the power and status of a leadership role and resist an accurate perception of organizational realities or themselves. They tend to disbelieve that their leadership is insufficient. Caught in a conundrum of their own making, they will not support change, even when the CEO insists it will happen. They will not openly admit that they are actively resisting, but they will do everything they can to avoid the experience, activities, and open communication that attend the organizational change process. They will do this while talking a minimally good talk. There is something going on here that is inimical to leadership. If it is not uncovered and stopped, it threatens to sabotage the project. The more central the leader, the more they are perceived as non-substitutable, the more dangerous the threat.

Consultant as Leader

How then does the consultant show leadership in dealing with this disruptive agent of the status quo? Organizations are often full of them. Peter Block has written about it eloquently in his classic, *Flawless Consulting* (2011). (My experience mostly echoes his.) For every progressive manager, there may be two or three who want to manage more than they want to lead. They might need coaching and even want it. They might be resisting what they do not understand. They might believe they should have a choice about whether to buy in to these new principles, values, mindsets, and management practices. At worst, they will perversely play-act obedience to the change, while resisting with every fiber of their being. The first three are O. K. and can be worked through with mutual engagement and accountability. It helps considerably if the climate supports constructive expression of conflict.

The CEO has to be willing to be a facilitator as well as an advocate. He might say, "Bring up your issues, and we'll talk it through. We'll seek common ground. We'll openly recognize our dilemmas. We'll treat them like the puzzles they are!" To deal with the adversary who will stop at nothing to undercut change and transformation, I advocate zero tolerance. It is like a bad infection that can make the whole patient sick again. That doesn't mean there aren't enemies of change who can be pragmatically restored to a position of contribution. I have seen them. Still, we would do well not to count on it. Sustainability of change requires that an institutionalization of the new norms and cultural practices occurs. Particularly while the organization is in cultural transition, it is essential that the power brokers of the old system be defanged. What does that mean? You decide. Just be clear that action is called for. Alongside this, I encourage the CEO to publically reaffirm the case for change and the values, goals, and road map being followed. When we talk about system-wide change, there is a fine balance to be obtained between freedom and participation. The tension is a function of a management and OD philosophy that argues, You are part of managing this change process. You are free to participate in the change process in ways uniquely appropriate to you and your group, and you are not free to undercut or inhibit the process, nor are you free to go through the motions with your boss, while criticizing the required involvement with your direct reports. The change process requires your open and committed involvement. The threat of sabotage is always there. We should be aware of that, remain alert, and ready to forestall it. That is change leadership.

Leadership, Character, and Relationships

What does it mean to be a leader? Surely it means to have a personal center that is not anchored in kryptonite (the element from Superman's home planet that brought him to his knees). Kryptonite symbolizes character traits that weaken us, cloud our judgment, tempt us to emotional outbursts, or cause us to be abusive to others. All of us have some kryptonite in our personal centers. The difference between a would-be leader and those content to follow is this: The leader has to take as their first and most important task the remaking of these habits and characteristics. In one sense, this is the qualification for the leadership post that most of us are least aware of. It does not appear on the job description. We are led to believe that experience, academic training, and a good track record is what should qualify us for leadership roles. Maybe we are good at managing budgets. Maybe we pushed through the university accreditation process in eighteen months. It is always something that we have done or some unique skill of ours that makes us a leader. All too often, we fail to acknowledge that what makes us effective leaders is our relationships with others (call them followers, direct reports, bosses, or stakeholders). These dynamically evolving relationships are what ultimately matters, and the traits and behaviors we bring from our previous lives to each particular existential moment punctuate these relationships.

Leaders are Always Developing

To be a leader or to take the lead means to accept the burden of knowing that we are now, as we stand, really inadequate to the job of leading others. Every other is different, and all of them want to be led differently (or not at all). The leader-follower transaction is a potential keg of dynamite, because it is frequently redefined by people in organizations as a matter of status and power. If someone is going to be a leader, someone else has to be a follower. Don't the two go together?

Thinking about leadership in this way is a great danger to organizations and their capacity for reaching higher levels of performance. A better way to see it: Leadership is a relationship where two or more people alternate in taking the lead to get a job or project accomplished. In our culture, none of us should saddle anyone else with the conceptual or practical burden of being a follower. Nonetheless, some leaders do more leading than others do, and some roles do call for more formal leadership behaviors. If you accept that leadership occurs in a reciprocal context, you will see that the leaders who have the most formal leadership responsibility also have the most responsibility for changing themselves. To be effective in leading change, formal leaders must model the ability to change both their mindsets and their external behavior. They must demonstrate that they perceive more of the complexity in life. They can live with the ambiguities occasioned by step-change. They can do this cognitively and emotionally.

What people need from us as leaders, when we are leading, is to see the external evidence of our growing and changing selves. Our partners across our networks need to see us act in ways that tell them that we are not fully predictable and always ready to surprise. We are aware of our limitations, yet constantly ready to say yes to the paradox and dilemmas of life. We are not just CEOs, vice-presidents, executives, and managers. We are leaders who see ourselves as part-of-the-problem-and-part-of-the-solution. It is a gestalt! (This is a wonderful quality in people; it takes a long time to develop; and, ironically, it may be the most difficult to find just when you need it the most.)

Confronting Prejudice

As managers, consultants, and employees, when the work of change becomes particularly difficult, we want to blame others for the things that go wrong. It is a natural tendency. At certain phases of the transformation process, we may find certain individuals and teams to be quite difficult for us. We want to control them out of existence. Fortunately, there is a window in time, as we attribute negative characteristics to others, where we can demonstrate our ability to grow and change deeply from within our personal centers. It ought to happen before the negative attribution has been socially shared with allies and reinforced; before, "Why can't so-and-so get on board?" becomes, "I'm not going to work with those idiots until they get their act together!" Once the other becomes an idiot, we have objectified, personalized, and distanced ourselves from a relationship of trust and respect. Although he or she may on some mean-spirited level be an idiot/obstacle for the personal ego, once we become bent on protecting our own vulnerability—which has been created by the attitude we have taken toward this person— we have lost the opportunity to build bridges and to help both of us change for the better. (I am not saying we all want to build bridges or that many of us are willing to change in the sense I am talking about. It takes a minimum of two people to build an interpersonal bridge. I am saying, stay open to the other and her seemingly distorted or difficult communications as long as you can. It sometimes takes a while for people to give up their charades and become real. Some never do, and that is tragic.) Ideally, we all ought to be able to identify with anyone we might meet in our organizational efforts, because they are all human beings with the potential for enacting the full spectrum of human behaviors. We are all kind, loving, decent, responsible, hostile, and vicious individuals at one time or another. When we forget that, and decide that some of us are much worse than others, we have begun to create a prejudice. Prejudice is prickly. It crowds out open inquiry. We all know where prejudice ultimately leads; just look at the history of mankind. (Racism is only the tip of the iceberg.)

As a leader, the important question to ask is, What can I do to prevent myself from becoming prejudiced toward those around me when the social psychological process of prejudice formation is so powerful and habit forming? What can I do when the flows of change seem to go on and on, and I'm feeling at loose ends with everyone and everything? Even the least little difference between us can, under the right circumstances, begin to justify why my attitude, job, gender, clothing, looks, intelligence, team, or homeland is better. We are all incipient misanthropes, in this sense. Our own lack of self-esteem drives us to play the one-upmanship game, and having gone down this path, we have left the path of leadership.

Leadership and Spiritual Awareness

There are universal, proven solutions to this problem of changing our character and ourselves in order to become better leaders and people. Many of them are spiritual or, increasingly today, psycho-spiritual. Some of the best can still be found within the framework of organized religion. (Let me hasten to add, one cannot flee to organized religion, sit in a pew, and passively wait for the manna from heaven to transform their lives. Heaven [spiritual fullness] tends to come to those who actively seek it!) All of these solutions have something meaningful to offer, and sometimes, often in desperation, executives and managers will seek them out.

What helps me to deal with dilemmas of leadership and character is to remind myself that we are all people—there is a lot of good, or potential good, in all of us—and that the person I am dealing with in particular has a lot of good traits, characteristics, attitudes, and behaviors.

I try to name them and think on them for a moment. At the same time, I work to detach from the negative thoughts and feelings which I have allowed to crystallize around my own perceptions and attitudes toward a fellow human being. In other words, I selectively perceive what we have in common, our humanity, and consciously choose to withdraw my attention from what I perceive we do not have in common, our differences. In addition, if I am still feeling annoyed at the person, I ask myself, Is there something I am still doing to fan the flames of antagonism in this relationship? Am I projecting a hated personal quality onto the other in order to cause myself to feel stronger, bigger, or more powerful? If the answer is yes, I try to stop doing it. I may also ask, Is there an element of self-pity or pride in my antagonism for this rival? (If I've called him/her a rival, I can be sure that my own motives are less than pure.) At the heart of this personal mastery process, I am acknowledging my own role in a relationship problem. I am refusing to project all my negative power onto the other. I am trying to find something to like in them, and I am cutting the negative knot that binds us together in a vicious circle of personal enmity. I work backward from my irrationality to a central, internal, psychological space characterized by intelligence and reason. If I can reach that place in my own personal center, half of the battle with myself (not the other) is won. If I can change myself, it will already have begun to have an impact on the other.

This is not Pollyanna stuff. This is using awareness and consciousness to drive out the unconscious, preconscious, and often irrational precursors of destructiveness in relationships. Leaders have the responsibility to do this more than others. This work is not easy, but it is essential. After all, how can you effectively lead those who you look down on, disparage, or alienate? They have already become an object to you, and the relationship element so necessary to leadership is missing.

Summary Propositions

I have attempted to characterize leadership from a more subjective point of view. In doing so, I have drawn on my own experience while realizing that your experience might be entirely different. In that sense, this is an existential analysis of leadership. Looking inward, we find that leaders and would-be leaders are often much more complex than we might imagine. How, then, do leaders deal with the fundamental problems of life that we all face, the problems of being and becoming? Here are seventeen propositions that may provide some answers. I hope that at the very least, they shed new light on the problem:

1. Leaders evolve by resolving existential dilemmas. Resolution implies that we accept the fact that we are human beings who are, in a very real sense, totally responsible for our decisions and ourselves.

2. A leader frequently has to choose between painful or unpleasant alternatives, knowing full well that the consequences cannot be predicted ahead of time and that they will have to live with whatever transpires. A leader faces the challenge, acts, and grows as a result. No matter what.

3. The choice to lead involves loneliness. The greater the leadership responsibility and the more wrenching the dilemmas, the more likely that one will feel, and be, alone with his choices. It is unavoidable.

4. The charisma our culture seems to look for in leaders is a false charisma. True charisma comes from facing one's depths.

5. We lead from our personal centers. When these are not very well developed, we will find our leadership efforts stymied.

6. Leadership potential can often erupt into activism when the situation is challenging and demands it (read the biography of Anwar Sadat).

7. Leadership behavior in the individual comes and goes. To keep the flame alive, you must develop your character.

8. Leadership is a universal trait. Let's stop calling people followers. In our culture, it has a negative connotation.

9. Leadership frequently means stepping out on faith. That is what it takes to resolve dilemmas.

10. Leaders derive strength of character from facing adversity as long as they maintain a certain spirit of humility in the process. They realize that the strongest leader can be undone by the qualities in which they are under-developed.

11. Leaders are learners. They do not accept surface definitions of problems and solutions. They probe and inquire.

12. Leadership transformation requires a great deal of self-awareness and the willingness to be disconfirmed, both by self and others.

13. The leadership of change requires personal transformation from all those who would lead. This requires both a willingness and an openness. The organization you are attempting to bring along is looking for it.

14. Leaders of change will confront saboteurs while inviting open discussion of motives and direction with those who are skeptical.

15. It is the quality of their relationships that make effective leaders. When these fail, or are bankrupt, it is often surprising how little can be done.

16. The broader the spectrum of human behavior and emotion with which the leader can identify, the more power they have to draw people to them. This very quality will help reduce parochial thinking in the organization and in society.

17. As the leader takes personal responsibility for driving out the destructive elements in their relationships, they signal a set of expectations to the people. These will speak louder than all the executive retreats and Covey (2000) workshops in China.

QUESTIONS FOR SELF-EXPLORATION

1. Are you convinced you are a very effective leader? Ask for some honest feedback from workers you trust and respect.

2. Write about the differences between following someone else's lead and taking the lead. Do a case analysis of when you performed these roles very well and then less well.

3. What character traits do you have that both enhance relationship building and that get in the way? Is there anything you need to do about either category?

REFERENCES

Bennis, W. G. & Nanus, B. (1997). *Leaders: Strategies for taking charge.* New York, NY: HarperBusiness.

Block, P. (1999). *Flawless consulting: A guide to getting your expertise used.* San Francisco: Jossey-Bass.

Churchill, W. S. (1991). *Memoirs of the Second World War [an abridgement].* Boston, MA: Mariner Books.

Cooper, R. K., & Sawaf, A. (1997). *Executive eq: Emotional intelligence in leadership and organizations.* New York, NY: Grosset/Putnam.

Eichinger, R. W. & Lombardo, M. M. (2007). *The leadership machine.* Los Angeles, CA: Korn/ Ferry.

Fiedler, F. E. (1981). *Leadership attitudes and group effectiveness.* Westport, CT: Greenwood.

Gilbert, M. (1995). *In search of Churchill: A historian's journey.* New York, NY: Wiley.

Kafka, F., (E. Muir & W. Muir, Trans.). (1995). *The trial.* New York, NY: Schocken Books.

Kierkegaard, S. (C. E. Moore, Trans.). (1999). *Provocations: spiritual writings of Kierkegaard.* Farmington, PA: Plough Publishing Company.

Klein, M. (1975). *The psycho-analysis of children.* New York, NY: Delacorte Press.

LeRoy, M. & Fleming, V. (1939). *The wizard of Oz.* United States: Metro-Goldwyn Mayer.

Nietzche, F. W. (W. Kaufmann, Trans.). (1995). *Thus spake Zarathustra.* New York, NY: Modern Library.

Nixon, R. M. (1962). *Six crises.* New York, NY: Doubleday.

Waite, R. G. L. (1997). *The psychopathic god: Adolf Hitler.* Portland, OR: Basic Books.

ON THE BANKRUPTCY OF KNOWLEDGE MANAGEMENT

Over the past three decades, global forces of competition have impacted all organizations, forcing managers to embrace strategy as a normative and guiding concept. Almost all of the larger organizations in the United States have gotten into the habit of regularly re-thinking their strategic plans. Small and medium-size firms have followed suit. What managers have learned from the social disciplines of organizational behavior and development is that implementing changes in strategy often means coming to terms with the existing culture of the organization. So increasingly, the two-to-three day exercise of creating the strategic plan has at the very least been conceptually wedded to organizational development approaches like Total Quality Management or Designing the High Performance Organization (Cummings and Worley 2009; Worley, Hitchin, and Ross 1996). Management now recognizes the critical role that organizational culture and working people play in the attainment of strategic shifts. It is their thoughts, attitudes, and behaviors which must shift if new strategies are to be enacted. One can see the same phenomenon at play in the information technology (IT) field. Strategies which are collectively known as Knowledge Management have proliferated across the industrial spectrum (See Wallace 2007). These involve the use of people, processes, and technology both to create new knowledge and to store existing knowledge in ways that make it accessible to the worker, 24/7. Managers in all sectors have learned that strategic thinking at the top does not automatically translate into new and more effective management practices throughout the system. There has to be an implementation plan, and that plan needs to be grounded in an understanding of organization development and information technology. Even so, while managers are more sophisticated today, they are sometimes all too willing to purchase a package that is nicely wrapped in ribbons, even when it smells like, looks like, and feels like a fad. As Dilbert (1996) would acknowledge, when the boss is looking, it is better to be seen doing something, no matter how ill informed, than to be pegged as lacking urgency. So the strategic change efforts have blossomed, the field research findings proliferate[1] and those whose jobs depend on the perception of change earnestly search for ways to reinforce that perception. In many cases, there was no institutionalization of the learnings which may have grown out of the numerous programs, but one might argue that there was enough success to keep executives interested.

Strategies for Organization Effectiveness

At the beginning of the millennium, a number of strategic perspectives emerged that seemed to have the potential for enhancing both the practice of management and the organization's strategic adaptability. These were: (1) Knowledge management, (2) intellectual capital theory, (3) strategic human resource management, and (4) organizational learning[2]. In the past, these domains of research and practice have

---

1 See O'Dell, Grayson, et. al. 1998; Wallace 2007; Worley, Hitchin, and Ross 1996

2 See Boxall and Purcell 2000; Brown and Woodland 1999; Crossan 1999; DeLong and Seeman 2000; Gannon, Flood, and Paauwe 1999; Gibb and Megginson 2000; Harrison 1998; Lee 2000; Mayo 2000; Narashima 2000; Wright 1998

had their separate proponents and schools of thought. Increasingly, however, all bodies of organization and management research are being loosely linked to the umbrella of organizational strategy and being subjected to the ironclad rule of the bottom-line: If you cannot measure it, it does not exist. Organizations are using approaches like the *Balanced Scorecard* (Kaplan and Morton 1996, 2001) to test the utility of current management practices that flow from theory and model-based strategies or professional bodies of knowledge. Finance and human resources departments are being asked to justify their goals, practices, and strategies. Increasingly, the question being asked is, What impact are you having on measures of organizational (firm) performance? Conceptual differentiation and elegance among the management disciplines is being traded for practical results. Impact on measurable organizational performance is becoming the decisive indicator of relevance[3].

In many ways, this sounds good. As with all trends, there is a positive side to it. When organizational ships are trying to map their way through challenging terrain, they need clear benchmarks and guidelines to tell them how they are doing. Unfortunately strategy has a way of breaking down in the details of implementation, and a one sided focus on bottom-line indicators can detract from the action learning elements of the strategic change process. Put another way, (1) if executives and managers want to know whether their organizations are becoming nimble in shifting strategies, (2) if they want to model what new strategic thinking and ongoing strategy implementation ought to look like, and (3) if they want to use that knowledge to hit the strategic target more often, then (4) they will have to do more than look at goal achievement and numerical indicators. The target will have to be recast and broadened, the net widened.

In this chapter, I propose that the strategic numbers focus, however well intended, has frequently been implemented in a counterproductive manner. What is gained in improved organizational performance comes at an excessive cost to the development of human capital and organizational learning. (That these last two matter will soon become apparent.) Researchers from divergent schools representing the topics of intellectual capital, knowledge management, organizational learning, and strategic human resource management perspectives all seem to recognize this, at both the conceptual and practical levels[4].

Gaps Between Strategy, Performance, and Numbers

To support my argument, I will focus on one of these topics, knowledge management (KM) and show how an excessive focus on measurement and the bottom-line tends to drive out the rich understandings that can come from an integration of thinking and practice across all four areas. I will show that these cross- disciplinary understandings are essential for the practicing managers who want to develop their organizations, their teams, and themselves.

---

3 See Boxall and Purcell 2000; Gannon, Flood, and Paauwe 1999; Gibbs and Megginson 2000; Mayo 2000; Wright 1998

4 Boxall and Purcell 2000; Crossan 1999; Delong and Seeman 2000; Gannon, Flood and Paauwe 1999; Gibb and Megginson 2000; Harrison 1998; Wright 1998; Narasimha 2000

I will argue directly, and by implication, that such development is necessary if organizations are to maintain any sort of strategic agility.

KM asks the question, How do we organize knowledge to improve organization learning and performance? KM tends to focus on the tools and techniques that enable organizations to collect, organize, and translate information into knowledge, which can be applied. Organizationally, KM applications are often located in the information technology (IT) department, under the direction of a chief technology officer (CTO) (Cummings and Worley 2009). Knowledge management has a measurement side, an information technology side, and a teamwork/collaboration side (O'Dell and Grayson 1998). As I will show, it tends to suffer from management's penchant to over measure and rely on technology investment as a silver bullet. As with other performance related activities, we are prone to measure before we are able to model a complex understanding of what knowledge management actually is (Jarboe 2007).

In the rest of this chapter I make the following arguments to support my point of view:

1. That societal forces interfere with the ability of executives and organizations to implement knowledge management;

2. That institutionalization of KM depends on organizational culture change and organizational learning;

3. That mechanistic thinking continues to prevail in many organizations;

4. That confusion over the definition of knowledge management, ambiguity about HR's role in the change process, and top management's understanding of organizational dynamics all lead to simplistic implementation plans (or to no plans at all).

5. I reflect on the recent economic downturn and explain how strategies like cost and people cutting drive out the knowledge sharing that must exist before knowledge management can occur.

6. Finally, drawing on an intellectual capital framework (Mayo 2000), I suggest steps to be taken to correct the one-sidedness of current management thinking.

Problems with Knowledge Management

Paradigm Conflict

A *Strategy and Leadership Roundtable Report* (1999) argued that "we are in the middle of a new culture war" (2) between those individuals who still subscribe to the paradigms of the Industrial Age and those who have entered, heart and mind, into the Knowledge Age. One might of course add that there are many people who are culturally divided in this sense. They carry a sort of cultural schizophrenia within; yet are forced to take a position as the turbulent forces of global competition accelerate. From this initial premise, it follows that there are culture wars going on in organizations, both within and between individuals. These wars limit the ability of executives to implement new knowledge management initiatives that will produce sustained competitive advantage. The article was written over a decade ago, but the insight still applies. In the more progressive Fortune 500 organizations, where many of the knowledge management programs were first started, this may have been less of an issue. Companies like BP and Buckman Laboratories were and are culturally homogeneous (Dixon

1995). They have taken great pains to ensure that the human resources they recruit subscribe to the norms and values of the Knowledge Age as institutionalized in their cultures. They have codified their knowledge orientation in the structures and systems of the company.

For Buckman Labs, that means that any employee, worldwide, has access to every other employee in bringing problem solving and best thinking to bear on customer- related issues. Technology, culture, and reward systems are aligned and integrated to reinforce the practice of knowledge sharing and the broadening of creative innovation that goes with it. In other Fortune 500 companies—K-Mart, for example— it seems clear that bureaucratic thinking, structures, and processes still exist (personal experience as a K-Mart customer). Not all of them, like K-Mart, may have filed for bankruptcy[5] but they are all at a distinct disadvantage in the struggle for industry preeminence and customer loyalty. Their outmoded organizations and cultures can stall or actively prevent the organizational and culture change required to institutionalize knowledge management.

Lack of Action

In midsize organizations with more of an entrepreneurial culture, one often finds the opposite type of problem. The author once worked for a software company that had reached the point in its growth and development where it could no longer rely on R&D management practices built around killer applications (Peters and Waterman 1982). It was now a global enterprise, and employees with valuable tacit knowledge (head knowledge about the business) were dispersed in far-flung locations. Theoretically, it should have been possible for employees to form ad hoc virtual teams around a particular new product design or customer problem. Most of them were familiar with the organizational culture and had been socialized to its values. Top management walked the halls of corporate, informally, and had even brought in consultants to help reengineer major work processes. People stayed at work late to work on projects and shared business knowledge on cross-functional teams. They understood software and customer expectations, and they had the technology for knowledge sharing. There was one essential that they lacked. At the senior executive level, they had been unable to make the leap from a conceptual understanding of what they meant by knowledge management to a well-organized strategic change process. Their espoused theory—what they said they believed—and their theory-in-use—what they actually did—were widely divergent (Argyris and Schon 1996) Over a two year period, a lot of time was devoted to the elucidation of a Knowledge Sharing White Paper, and the president of the organization published a well-received article on the need for finding ways to transfer valuable tacit knowledge from a large group of employees who were getting ready to retire to the next generation of managers and employees. What top management had failed to do was to develop a knowledge management action plan that had all levels of management committed to decision and action steps until they were up to their eyeballs in real-time implementation of strategy. Even after fifty years of successful organizational development theory and practice, this is still not unusual in organizations. As managers, we often know what works, but we do not do it!

---

5   CNNMoney 2002, ¶ 1

Crossan, in her comprehensive review of the organizational learning literature has argued that knowledge management is an important organizational strategy (1999). She would agree it is essential to competitive strength. Conversely, a major criticism she has leveled at companies is that they focus too much on cognitive complexity and too little on action taking when designing and implementing programs like knowledge management.

The role of experience in the development of shared understanding reinforces the learning premise that cognition (knowledge, understanding, and beliefs) and action (behaviors) are tightly intertwined. In real-time strategy implementation, changes in knowledge do not necessarily lead to changes in action. In contrast to knowledge management and intellectual capital, which focus management and research attention on cognition, this view of organizational learning acknowledges the rich interrelationship between cognition and action.

Her thesis fits David Kolb's model of experiential learning (1984). This now classical theory argues that there are four phases in the individual or organizational learning cycle. To use the example of individual learning, a person is in a real world situation and has an experience (called Concrete Experience in the Kolb model). They then reflect on the ways in which this experience may relate to other experiences or try to look at it from the point of view of the other actors involved (Reflective Observation). The next step is to incorporate their observations into a conceptual framework, a theory which can be tested through action (Abstract Conceptualization). Then the individual acts to test their hypotheses (Active Experimentation) and is once again back in the world of Concrete Experience. Kolb would say that learning does not fully occur unless the individual has completed all four phases of the cycle.

The difficulty with initiatives like knowledge management often lies at the executive and strategic levels where learning-which-leads-to-action could reasonably be expected to occur. Too often we find thinkers there who are preoccupied with other priorities and unable to model what this type of action learning would look like. They may be action oriented in the areas of the business they understand, but they frequently rely on consultants to tell them what to do in the ambiguous arena that Lev calls the utilization of intangible assets (2001).

Deferring to Human Resources

Organizational knowledge is an intangible asset; human capital is an intangible asset. To the executive mind, notable exceptions aside, these domains normally fall within the province of strategic human resource management (SHRM). If change is to occur, the VP of Human Resources should be the driver. The problem, aside from the obvious one that that executives are not learning to lead organizational change (Lee 2000) is that human resource executives are just as frequently unlikely to be focused on the needs of people and the criticality of balancing those needs with external demands and the expectations of top management. They, too, have other priorities.

Strategic human resource management as a field was arguably born in 1980 when Devanna, Fombrum, and Tichy wrote a seminal article, "Human Resources Management: A Strategic Perspective." During the last thirty years, HR managers and practitioners have been struggling to gain credibility in a more strategic role. The latest challenge has been to demonstrate to top management how they contribute, meaningfully and metrically, to the organization's sustainable competitive advantage. This is surely a worthwhile mission. For a mature profession, self-assured and aware of its role in the Knowledge Age, it could be done. The problem is that in many organizations HR has not gained sufficient trust and commitment from management to partner effectively with them; there are many exceptions in top tier organizations, but in this case, the exceptions prove the rule (Becker, Huselid, and Ulrich 2001; Rothwell, Prescott, and Taylor 1998). Not necessarily the fault of the profession or of individuals within it, the fact remains that HR may not be well-positioned to lead major change initiatives such as those required by knowledge management programs. Executives like Jack Welch of General Electric have partnered well with Human Resources and argued that the senior HR executive needs to be "elevated to a position of primacy and power in the organization (2005, 99)." Jack was, of course, an executive who had achieved the highest stature. This makes the point even more solidly. In his case, he valued highly what the "best HR types" could do and used their services to implement TQM and other change initiatives at General Electric. It is even truer, however, that he expected executive commitment to leadership and action outside of the HR function. As CEO, Jack Welch took a strongly personal interest in seeing that his model of people and business differentiation got implemented throughout GE. For him, strategy meant executive commitment, action, learning, and performance. You could partner with HR, but you could not abrogate your executive leadership responsibilities. If this is the testimony of one of the most wildly successful executives of our time—someone who spoke from experience, not theory—how much more likely is this to be true in organizations where HR is still building its credibility?

Conceptual Confusion

If strategic human resources management is only beginning to come into its own, the literature on knowledge management suggests that there is no widely accepted definition or a well-developed research and practice base for this field. Diane Sinclair (2000) in the practitioner-oriented journal *People Management* has stated that

> Knowledge management is an ambiguous term. People interpret the concept in different ways. For some, knowledge management is concerned with the introduction of company intranets or other technical ways of improving the flow of information. For others, it is a range of management activities aimed at developing and exploiting knowledge, with important social, political and economic considerations.[6]

Mayo (1998) argues that knowledge management is building on what is known and extending it into future projects. Roy Harrison (1998), of the Institute for Personnel and Development's Research Project on Knowledge Management, argues that knowledge management is an essential component of learning organizations. (I have already referred to the organizational learning theorist, Mary Crossan, who stated that understanding what

---

6   2000, November 9. An investigative approach. 6, 22, 75

organizational learning actually is would help knowledge management practitioners get beyond the quagmire of cognition) (1999). Interestingly, this condition has a parallel in academic analysis paralysis. Maybe professional practitioners, corporate executives, and business and academic consultants all need to reframe their strategy implementation methods to focus on action? Do we need to understand before we act? Sometimes simple models of the situation that lead to early action can increase our understanding to the point where strategic action becomes focused, comprehensive, and effective. No one is spinning his or her wheels.

Brown and Woodland, in a case study of a pharmaceuticals plant in Great Britain, argue that knowledge management ought to mean retaining the tacit, irreplaceable knowledge of the organization's knowledge workers (1999). They cite the example of Henry Blake, an expert microbiologist who retired from a company where there was no managerial effort or plan to retain his knowledge. His knowledge base was unique, and there was the potential for an immediate and sustainable negative impact on the bottom-line.

Allport (1924) and Douglas (1986) have questioned the usefulness of phrases like organizational learning and knowledge management. They argue that these are extensions of terms that apply only to the individual. Other than their purpose as convenient referents, we have no idea whether they exist (Narasimha 2000). Alternately, Sandelands, and Stablein (1987) note that the three criteria for the existence of mind—a physical substrate, capable of encoding ideas, and permitting complex interactions among them—all have equivalents at the organizational level of analysis (124). These are: Computer hardware [substrate], computer software [encoding ideas], and complex computer programs [capable of cross-communication]. Worth noting is that we have come full circle in the complex knowledge sharing that currently exists in our web-based learning portals[7].

Lee (2000) distinguishes between data, information, and knowledge. Knowledge is information which has been "embedded and synthesized in the brain" (35). He blatantly identifies it as intellectual capital and argues that it is difficult to "communicate, structure, or capture electronically":

> Knowledge by its very nature is highly personal and extremely difficult to transfer with richness as complete as the original holder of the knowledge understands it. This difficulty in transfer is what often makes knowledge tacit as opposed to explicit (as data is). What distinguishes knowledge from its data and information brethren is the inclusion of the human contribution, and hence more value to the transferee. It is also distinguished by its closeness to the application of its use [i.e., context] (34).

Why does all this matter? In the absence of a clear consensus on what organizational learning and knowledge management are, or what they look like, there is no real way to determine their role and contribution to organizational adaptation and performance. They could be proxy terms for a more or less complex model of reality that might have increased utility for executives, practitioners, and academics.

---

7 Author's observation, January 11, 2016

Political Perspectives

Delong and Seeman (2000) look at it somewhat differently. For them, knowledge management is the development of tools, processes, systems, structures, and cultures in order to improve the creation, sharing, and use of knowledge essential to organizational decision-making (33). Their major contribution is not their definition. They have developed a penetrating analysis of the conceptual confusion around KM that is worth elaborating on. First, they note that many companies do not know what KM is (34). They argue that this ambiguity lends itself to placing KM in whatever conceptual category the sponsors happen to be familiar with. They cite the example of a company that implemented a knowledge management initiative by piggybacking it onto their long-standing reengineering program (33). With an excessive focus on performance and measurement, they drove KM through the organization, ignoring the need to facilitate organizational learning through dialogue, reflection, and debate. This is a good example of how a potentially powerful and organic process of cultural development was forced to embrace a mechanistic implementation methodology. Political conflict emerged, and the organization was the loser. The organization had no doubt learned that knowledge management was a joke.

Delong and Seeman distinguish between four central perspectives on knowledge management: (1) Strategy/leadership; (2) knowledge content/practice; (3) technology; and (4) change management/reengineering (35–26). They argue that all four perspectives are required to effectively design and implement knowledge management programs. What they found in their consulting work was substantial variation within each perspective and a failure to fully acknowledge and appreciate the other perspectives. For example, strategy/leadership proponents may take either a reengineering or behavioral science view of change management. The point is, Whatever leadership's position, it will influence their ideas for implementing knowledge management. In the real world that these practitioner researchers inhabit, knowledge management has remained *ambiguous and multi-faceted, subject to a range of interpretations.* This frequently leads to overly simplistic, one-sided approaches. What is the lesson? In the strategic implementation of knowledge management programs, the assumptions, values, and cognitive maps of the various stakeholder perspectives need to be surfaced and synthesized into a shared vision of what KM can and should be for a particular organization (36). Without this political sensitivity, knowledge management programs will lose their impact as ideological coalitions fight to bring this domain and the organizational resources committed to it into their own political camps.

The Politics of Organizational Change

To summarize, if senior leadership is frequently unclear about knowledge management and their own role in institutionalizing KM programs, and if the domain itself is fraught with complexity, multiple meanings, and political infighting, how might one expect strategic human resource managers to lead implementation efforts? My hypothesis—as a manager, teacher, and consultant—is that HR executives, in an effort to gain credibility and influence with top management, have embraced concepts like intellectual capital, knowledge management, and the Balanced Scorecard (Kaplan and Norton 2001). This commitment has been superficial, but energetic, and it will wax and wane with the political winds blowing from the offices of senior management. This is not a criticism. If the executive leaders of the organization were taking primary responsibility for embedding knowledge management into the culture, then HR managers would have a context for success. Where that does not exist, about the best they can do is to continue to chip away at executive intransigence and perhaps champion significant initiatives in their own functional areas. What they should not attempt to do is "go it alone" without significant executive or consulting support.

Knowledge Turned Inward

If strategic human resource management is an incomplete answer for implementing knowledge management, it is even truer that in times of economic downturn—like we have faced globally since 2007—knowledge sharing, the acknowledged precursor to knowledge management, will suffer. Rapid response thinking (what we all tend to do when things seem to be going south) frequently causes organizations to adopt short-term strategies like cost and personnel cutting to maintain profits and productivity and ensure survival. In such a business and social climate, the psychological contract between employee and company is further eroded or broken (Rosseau 1995). Trust deteriorates as expectations for equity and ethics in the workplace are put to the test by seemingly unfeeling executive decisions. Job-related knowledge sharing is displaced by knowledge sharing for personal survival. Employees share information about job leads outside the organization, and as large companies announce wave after wave of layoffs, fear and desires for self-protection cause the survivors to hoard whatever knowledge they might possess to press into the service of their own career planning[8] . In part, this is the new psychological contract between employer and employee (Osland, Kolb, and Rubin 2001). Employees have learned that they are fully responsible for their own careers, and Generation Xers have determined that work is not even their first priority. Commitment is abrogated; relationships become transactional, and no hard feelings. Paradoxically, this phenomenon is occurring during the time when we are just beginning to understand what it takes to manage intangibles such as knowledge. Since knowledge is ultimately created and used by human beings, there is no way to manage it without taking human needs and aspirations into account. Organizations may incentivize employees to share their tacit knowledge with each other, and they may want to engage the whole person (Wallace 2007; O'Dell and Grayson 1998). Still, if the psychological contract is primarily based on a tentative and short-term bargaining relationship, management will have difficulty generating the level of commitment required for institutionalization. It does not matter that sixty percent of the employees are still working for the company. When short-term cost containment and productivity gains become the sole criteria for organization effectiveness or success, then the organization is beginning to lose its soul. (Soul in this sense is not a technical term. Instead, it captures the rending of the organizational fabric, which occurs when employee stayers are left behind to pick up the pieces.)

---

8   Author's personal interviews with employees of Fortune 500 companies, 2010–2015

Implications for Managers

As one might expect, the news from the trenches is not all bad. Focusing on organizational effectiveness and performance has been a profitable discipline and not just in a monetary sense. Estimates are that intangible assets represent about eighty-four percent of the financial assets in the corporate sector (Jarboe 2015). Across the country, thoughtful and adventurous executives have spent billions of dollars on employee development. They want to know that their investment is creating value or wealth added through people (Mayo 2000). It could be argued that concepts like value-added have helped fuel the global spread of capitalism during the last few decades. So while I have decried the excessive emphasis on metrics and performance, it is still true that profit making organizations do exist to create wealth for their shareholders. In today's economy that may include many of their own employees. This profit sharing in the newer sense means that financial inequities within and between companies can be at least partially redressed by the hand of the marketplace. In good times, more and more employee investors win. In down times, they share the fate of other shareholders (excluding top management, unless you include personal buy-outs as a type of fate). It is unclear how the large numbers of underemployed knowledge and blue-collar workers will ultimately affect productivity in the workplace. We do know that many employees who are left behind complain of burnout in the face of overall workloads that have not been reduced. We also know that when there is an oversupply of sellers (the individuals who contract the use of their skills and service abilities), there is often a tendency for management to work less at employee relations because in hard times, it is frequently seen as a gratuitous display of good will that "we simply cannot afford!" To put it somewhat differently, "Let them eat cake!" (overstated as a point of contrast with the underutilized aspects of human potential and personal investment that create the vaunted value-added).

I am not against performance and metrics, but I am against their obsessive utilization as measures of value or worth. I believe that people are infinitely resilient and that their psychological growth and development should be fostered because it is the right thing to do. It is a longer-term investment that will also lead to short-term results. While most people cannot be controlled into commitment, many do want to do the best they can for their organization, work group, and customer base. They often want to be measured against goals that they themselves help to establish. It has something to do with self-esteem and the drive for competence. I believe people should be valued as human beings first and as employees second. This makes pragmatic business sense as well as being a corporate responsibility value for many organizations (Starbucks, et. al. 2015). If management adopted this attitude and behaved accordingly, most employees would produce results that exceed expectations.

That said, I am certain that my beliefs may seem a bit one-sided to some: Am I just another wide-eyed idealist? Earlier in my career, I would have been guilty as charged. In 2016, I believe that the best organizations have validated my thinking. Besides, in our age of discontinuity, idealism and pragmatism are not necessarily opposites. They have become part of a wheel of sustainability. Business values can no longer be separated from human values. That does not make me a bleeding heart. It makes me a realist. The old dichotomies are crumbling in the face of new global challenges.

Leading in an Age of Ambiguity

What should change leaders do to create and sustain the effective management of knowledge in an age of culture wars, global dislocation, and transitory commitments? I recommend applying Andrew Mayo's theory of developing employees to grow human capital, as described in the human resources journal, *Personnel Review* (2000). Mayo believes that the Industrial Age practice of reviewing economic value added in financial formula is incomplete. He argues that people are the drivers of value and that we cannot even begin to understand value added until we have a clear definition of intellectual capital and the management of intangibles. Using the standard equation, Market value = Tangible assets + Intangible assets, Mayo believes that we have a preliminary high-level definition of intellectual capital. It is the sum of the intangibles in an organizational system. More specifically, he cites the following three domains as the essential elements of intellectual capital:

» customer (external structural) capital, e. g., customer contracts, relationships, loyalty, and satisfaction; market-share; image; reputation; brands;

» organizational (internal structural) capital; e. g. systems, methodologies, patents, know-how, databases, knowledge, culture;

» human capital, e. g., individual competence and experience, judgment, wisdom, team competence, leadership, and motivation (253).

In this elaboration we can clearly see that Mayo is not at all uncomfortable with the soft side of intellectual capital. Yet he goes even further to enunciate a principle that has direct implications for knowledge management, change management, and change leadership:

All intellectual assets are maintained and grown by people. [People] are the source of all components. Their unique contribution comprises their command of information and previous experience, their ability to integrate and use judgment, to be innovative and intuitive, and to develop and use human relationships. This contribution we could label knowledge in the widest sense and see its continual creation and its flow around the organization [and across the supply chain] as the vital dynamic of progress. The constant generation of new knowledge and experience and its availability for the benefit of all who can use it effectively, are fundamental issues. Arguably the most important of all business processes are those designed to accomplish these tasks, and the role of employee development takes on a specifically strategic mantle as a primary means of achieving these goals (Mayo 2000).

Mayo has a theory of management, human behavior, and human effectiveness embedded in his model (522–534). It is consistent with the central arguments of this chapter. It balances the need for value creation with the need for employee development. It takes into account all three domains of intellectual capital: (1) customer relations and commitment, (2) organization structure, and culture, and (3) experienced, competent and creative people.

If KM is to have any hope as a viable program or strategy, it will have to incorporate these guidelines into its mission:

1.   It is the job of management to develop intellectual capital. (This means customer, organizational, and human assets.)

2.   Managers and employees need to measure what they do in terms of a full spectrum of outputs. (Number of training sessions will not cut it.)

3.   Everyone needs to use indicators that can show trends up or down. (To manage knowledge or anything else, we need to know where our efforts are taking us over time.)

4.   Human capital is difficult to quantify, yet we must try.

5.   Human capital needs to be grown and developed in order to add value.

6.   This is a model of human development that includes individual capability, motivation, leadership, organizational climate, and work group effectiveness, dynamically interacting. Each of these needs to be grown in order to produce a synergistic impact on human value added.

7.   The primary question for managers should be: Is this activity/person contributing positively to future value-creation or not?

8.   Individual, team, and organizational development are in the direct line of value creation and the strategic goals of the organization. (Management is creating intellectual capital by fostering the practices that produce measurably superior outcome performance.)

QUESTIONS FOR SELF-EXPLORATION

1. What are you as a manager and leader doing to build the intellectual and knowledge capital of your organization and its employees?

2. How do you perceive your employees? Are they valuable resources, interchangeable parts, or something else?

3. Do you know the amount of tacit, or work related knowledge that your employees carry around in their heads? Do you know how to motivate them to use it? Will it matter if they don't?

REFERENCES

Agryris, C. & Schön, D. (1974). *Theory in practice: Increasing professional effectiveness.* San Francisco: Jossey-Bass.

Agyris, C. & Schön, D. A. (1996). *Organizational learning II: Theory, methods, and practice.* Menlo Park, CA: Addison-Wesley.

Boxall, P. & Purcell, J. (2000). Strategic human resource management: Where have we come from and where should we be going? *International Journal of Management Reviews, 2,* 183–204.

Brown, R. B. & Woodland, M. J. (1999). Managing knowledge wisely: A case study in organizational behaviour. *Journal of Applied Management Studies, 8,* 175–199.

Conger, J. A. (2001). How 'Gen X' managers manage. In J. S. Osland, D. A. Kolb & I. M. Rubin, (Eds.), *The organizational behavior reader* (pp. 9–20) Upper Saddle River, NJ: Prentice-Hall.

Cotter, J. J. (1995). *The 20% solution: Using Rapid Resign™ to create tomorrow's organizations today.* New York, NY: Wiley.

Crossan, M. M. (1999). An organizational learning framework: From intuition to institution. *Academy of Management Review, 24,* 522–538.

Cummings, T. G., & Worley, T. G. (2009). *Organization development & change.* Mason, OH: Southwestern Cengage Learning.

Delong, D. & Seemann, P. (2000). Confronting conceptual confusion and conflict in Knowledge Management. *Organizational Dynamics, 29,* 33–45.

Dixon, N.M. (2000). *Common knowledge: How companies thrive by sharing what they know.* Boston, MA: Harvard Business School Press.

Douglas, M. (1986). *How institutions think.* New York, NY: Syracuse University Press.

Gannon, M., Flood, P., & Paauwe, J. (1999). Managing human resources in the third era: Economic perspectives. *Business Horizons. 42,* 41–48.

Gibb, S. & Megginson, D. (2000). (Eds). Power, person, and process in the new employee development. *Personnel Review, 29,* 438–445.

Harrison, R. (1998). Intellectual assets. *People Management, 4,* 33–34.

Jacobs, R. W. (1994). *Real time strategic change: How to involve an entire organization In fast and far-reaching change.* San Francisco, CA: Berrett-Koehler.

Kmart files Chapter 11. (January 22, 2002). CNNMoneySM. Retrieved from http://money.cnn.com/2002/01/22/companies/kmart/

Kaplan, R. S. & Norton, D. P. (1996). *The balanced scorecard: Translating strategy into action.* Boston, MA: Harvard Business School Press.

Kolb, D. A. (1983). *Experiential learning: Experience as the source of learning and development.* Englewood Cliffs, NJ: Prentice-Hall.

Lee, J., Sr. (2000). Knowledge Management: The intellectual revolution. *IIE Solutions, 32* (10), 34–38.

Lev, B. (2001). Intangibles: Now more important than ever. *Harvard Business Review, 3* (5), 7–9.

Levitt, B. & March, J. G. (1988). Organizational learning. *Annual Review of Sociology, 14,* 319–340.

Mayo, A. (2000). The role of employee development in the growth of intellectual capital. *Personnel Review, 29* (4), 521–534.

Narashima, S. (2000). Organizational knowledge, human resource management, and sustained competitive advantage: Toward a framework. *Competitiveness Review, 10,* 123–136.

Peters, T. J. & Waterman, R. H. (2004). *In search of excellence.* New York, NY: HarperBusiness.

Polyani, M. (1967). *The tacit dimension.* New York, NY: Doubleday.

Rousseau, D.M. The psychological contracts: Violations and modifications. In J. S. Osland, D. A. Kolb & I. M. Rubin, (Eds.), *The organizational behavior reader* (pp. 2–9) Upper Saddle River, NJ: Prentice-Hall.

Sandelands, L.E., Hamel, G. (1987), The concept of organizational mind. In S. Bacharach & N. DiTomaso (Eds.), *Research in the sociology of organizations: Vol. 5* (pp. 135–162) Greenwich, CT: JAI Press.

Seely-Brown, I. & Duguid, P. (1991) Organizational learning and communities of practice: Toward a unified view of working, learning, and innovation. *Organizational Science, 2,* 40–57.

Senge, P. *The fifth discipline: the art and practice of the learning organization.* New York, NY: Doubleday/Currency.

Shrivastva, P. (1983). A typology of organizational learning systems. *Journal of Management Studies, 20,* 7–28.

Sinclair, D. (2000, November 9). An investigative approach. *People Management, 6,* 22, 75. The role of business in the 21st Century: A strategy and leadership roundtable. *Strategy and Leadership, 27* (4/5), 26–31.

Trist, E. & Baumforth, K. W. (1951). Some social and psychological consequences of the long wall method of coal getting. *Human Relations, 4,* 3–38.

Walsh, J. P. (1995). Managerial and organizational cognition: Notes from a trip down memory lane. *Organization Science, 6,* 280–321.

Weick, K. (1979). *The social psychology of organizing.* Reading, MA: Addison-Wesley.

Worley, C. G., Hitchin, D. E., & Ross, W. L. (1996). *Integrated strategic change: How OD builds competitive advantage.* Reading, MA: Addison-Wesley.

Wright, P. M. (1998). Introduction: Strategic human resource management research in the 21st Century. *Human Resource Management Review, 8* (3), 187–192.

MAPPING THE REAL ORGANIZATION

The purpose of this chapter is (1) to explain how we impose our unique cognitive frames on our interpersonal experiences, (2) to show how interpersonal behavior in organizations tends to be self-reinforcing, and (3) to illustrate how we make judgments and draw conclusions that are rarely tested. One fundamental reason for the way we view relationship issues is our desire to think well of ourselves and save face. I will show how our own desire to justify ourselves to self and others creates barriers to the vaunted task-oriented behaviors all organizations applaud but so rarely see in any pure and untainted form.

I start by defining the concept vicious circle and provide an example of how one is created. (I did not invent the term—see Senge 1990—my definition and usage have been constructed to reinforce the central message of this book.) I demonstrate how the layers of hostile and self-protective interpretation of others' behavior can lead to conflict and communications breakdowns. Finally, I tie this to the current norms of doing business, made worse by the pressured uncertainty generated by global competition. Particularly in the business world, we thrive on creating verbal short-hand, finding rapid closure to conversations, generalizing beyond the data, and making quick judgments, rather than trying to understand, empathize, or appreciate (Vickers 1995). This environment is the breeding ground for vicious circles. Task-oriented norms assume that people are rational, that feelings and emotions can probably be ignored, and that what does not get expressed probably does not matter. I will show how this attitude leads to dysfunction and how it reduces the organization's ability to complete its priority tasks.

In the second half of this chapter, I make the point that healthy organizations can be conceptualized as overlapping matrices of virtuous circles. These get created when individuals act with openness and integrity and when they do not allow personal slights or wounds to over-determine their behavior and actions. The foundation for this is trust and risk-taking. There has to be the ability to perceive everyday life in our organizations and our own selves in fresh and spontaneous ways. The steps to beginning a virtual circle are:

1. Viewing of self as an individual with integrity who keeps his promises;
2. Avoiding premature judgment of the other, looking for positive elements in the behavior and character of others;
3. Knowing that everyone makes mistakes—but not using that as a personal excuse to keep making the same ones—and most importantly;
4. Acting on these beliefs and assumptions.

Organizations produce Annual Reports but often don't find it necessary to discuss the small ways in which we let each other down while going about the business of performing our jobs. It is these undiscussed violations of expectations that create destructive communication patterns (Rousseau 1995).

On Circular Reactions

In Chapter Two, I spoke of organizations as blossoms and urged a nonlinear experimentation upon those of us who would understand organizations (practically all of us; our well-being depends upon it). Another symbol of organizational life is the circle or curvilinear line that closes back upon itself. The circle or some variant of it is useful to help us think about holistic properties of organizations. Many elements of organizational communication are circular, in the sense that they begin somewhat innocently, even arbitrarily, and then begin to generate momentum, energy, and force. Two excellent examples are vicious and virtuous circles. Vicious circles are patterns of hostile interaction caused by one person (or group) taking a negative action, which then causes another person or group to retaliate in kind. This causes the first party to reciprocate, and so on (Watzlawick et.al. 1967). You won't find these organizational dynamics in any annual report, and yet the barriers which build up between individuals, groups, departments, and organizations, can often by explained by these vortices of negativity. They are invisible to the naked eye, yet easily perceived by an insightful actor who becomes part of the organization.

Organization development consultants and most managers are quite familiar with vicious circles. There is a whole language that lets you know you have stepped into the middle of one. For example, statements like, "You know the admin people; they just don't get it!" or, "Yeah, we're all supposed to support the new vision except for my boss; guess the rules don't apply to her." Most vicious circles start with interactions that have broken down, where the expectation of mutuality has been violated, and where individuals begin to make judgments about the other, their ability and integrity.

The Power of Vicious Circles

For example, you and I know each other. I see you in the hall and say hello to you. You see me but instead of saying hello you look quickly away and start talking to your neighbor who is at your right hand. We have both taken an action, and now each of us is free to impose an interpretation upon our own action **and** the other's. I might think, "What's with Julie? I've known her for years and she snubs me in the hall! You will note that I have based my appraisal of the meaning of her action solely upon my own observation, within my own cognitive frame for Ms. X and what she means to me. I have not stopped to ask her why she might have failed to say hello or considered that my interpretation of her behavior might have been totally off base. In fact, it is in the nature of my part business, part friendly relationship with Julie that we rarely communicate about our communication process (called meta-communication). Instead, we take our communication and its meaning for granted, assuming that we both understand our own motives and intentions as well as those of the other. Often, we stereotype both ourselves and the other person in a series of fleeting moments: "John just doesn't pay attention." "You know, Sue really thinks she's hot stuff." or "Who does he think he is?" It may take more than one set of interactive behaviors to trigger stereotyping or hostile generalizations, but note that the situation is frequently exacerbated by an organizational climate or context of negativity that reinforces our own skewed perceptions of a particular interaction. For example, the planning department is frequently angry with the operations manager, based on a series of behavioral incidents that has escalated into virtual circles of swirling conflict. As more and more parties step into this cloud of hostile interpretation, a context gets created which will prejudice and predispose individual actors from both groups to see the other group in an unfriendly and hostile way.

I won't even need to have interacted with you before labeling you as unreliable. My colleague has assured me that you are, and I implicitly assume that he or she has based his inferences on observable, behavioral data. In other words, in typical interactions in work organizations, we frequently take a lot for granted. We assume much about meaning, context, and intention, both for ourselves and others. Of course, we make assumptions in a lot of other contexts as well, but in work organizations, with norms of task completion and the desire to maintain face (Lemert and Branaman 1997), the tendency to operate on incomplete data is rampant. We believe the situation demands it. We are driven.

Back to my example: Suppose Julie has seen me say hello to her, but at the same time, the person to her right (John) has made a pressing remark that demands her attention. She wants to acknowledge me, but feels the insistent press to respond to her colleague. Julie cocks her head to the right and starts to speak, perhaps thinking, "I really have to find a way to acknowledge Jeff over there. I have not seen him in some time, but that will have to wait until I take care of John." By the time she has taken care of John, she is fifty yards down the hall and may have forgotten about me. Yet I may have taken offense at what I perceived to be a violation of my expectations. Sometimes small incidents such as this are enough to set the stage for the creation of a vicious circle.

To the extent that both Julie and I are willing to meta-communicate about what happened, it may be possible to stop the process before it begins to draw energy. But she and I are both busy; we hold at least several hundred conversations a day. How likely is it that either of us will attempt to repair this one? It is not that we do not care. It is that organizational communication thrives on shorthand and rapid closure. Generalizing beyond the data and rendering personal judgments based on inadequate data are forms of interpersonal and perceptual shorthand. Were it not for the fact that we are dealing with human beings who possess self-concepts and perceptual limitations designed to enhance their self-images, all might be well. If Ann had a little bit better image of herself and I, in turn, were less thin-skinned in evaluating her behavioral intention (which, in truth, I had no way of knowing) then maybe the tendency for communications to break down in vicious circles could be prevented. However, Ann is defensive about receiving feedback from anyone, and I am known for rendering judgments at the drop-of-a-hat. There you have it—the beginning of a vicious circle. If I cement it by refusing to make eye contact in the lunchroom—a nonverbal coup d' grace—we may have invited each other to a dance without end (Watzlawick, et. al. 1967).

If this does not sound like your organization, very good. You are to be congratulated for demonstrating maturity and restraint. However, it is worth noting that vicious circles are the intangible substance of many organizations. They overlay and interpenetrate different departments and individuals in the forms of energy blocks and organizational stuck points. Constructive action and completion of work is frequently stalled. It is not that work does not get done—there is, in fact, a bottom-line—it is just that it gets performed less effectively or efficiently. If you could actually see these vicious circles, they would tell you more about what is going on than all the organizational charts in the world.

Virtuous Circles

What then of circles as positive symbols? In addition to vicious circles, there are virtuous circles. These are circular patterns of interaction which reinforce and augment one another and which lead to changes in climate and context that are positive for human beings, their growth, and bottom-line results. For example, suppose I am your direct report, and you are my boss. Whenever I interact with you in the following way, I am beginning to create a virtuous circle: (a) You invite me into your office; (b) you are angry that a report of mine is overdue; (c) although I feel foolish being reprimanded, I stand and take my punishment; (d) instead of making excuses, I admit the error of my ways, and most importantly, I really listen and note that what you are angry about is not the lateness (I was only one day late) but that I did not let you know ahead of time that I was not going to meet the deadline. In fact, I had not spoken with you for over a week, leaving you with the assumption that everything was on target. Here, as with the vicious circle above, an expectation was violated. In this case, however, both parties begin to meta-communicate about the broken sets of expectations: If I have learned to tolerate anger as something other than a unilateral message—its meaning is often complicated—I may be able to summon up the courage to paraphrase back something to the effect that, "You're really angry about my not staying in touch with you on this very important project." If he/she says something like, "You're darn right I am!" you could follow-it-up with, "Look I apologize; I know I deserve this, and yes, I did know how important it was to stay in close touch with you on this project. I let other priorities get in my way. Thank you for holding me accountable." Trying to protect your backside, whether you have made a legitimate or an illegitimate mistake is often begging the question. Communications problems in organizations tend to be circular in nature. Often it is not a question of competence but of the perceived integrity of the other. Assuming a minimal level of competence, are you someone I can trust to meet their obligations? Will you acknowledge your mistakes? Are you a con artist or a straight shooter? If, in any given interaction, you can impress the other individual as one who is conscientious, reliable, and willing to tell the truth, you have created the makings of a virtuous circle.

Circular Patternings

In the case of vicious circles, hundreds of hostile interactions bring closure to a circle of animosity and destruction. It is, in fact, a part of the organizational architecture, whether tangible or not. You can run into it when trying to get two departments to work better together. Where there is a long history of distrust and animosity, you will find that vicious circles have crystallized into walls. Layers of tension and defenses have been used to cement the bricks of resentment. And underneath it all, at the core, is a series of communications that signaled, "You are not a person I can trust or do business with." That was the implicit meta-communication, no matter what the original content of the messages.

Alternatively, virtuous circles begin to create and symbolize the bringing of closure to a series of mutually enhancing interactions. The precipitate of these discussions can also be felt in organizations and in another sense *are* organizations. When hundreds of people are beginning to follow through on their promises, it creates a circular, holistic context for every single interaction that occurs within the organizational boundaries. Finding out I can trust an individual or a group of people, I begin to relax my defenses and can then allow myself to be more open and honest. I do not have to defend myself against their expected judgments and criticisms. I take responsibility for completing my part of the virtuous circle, which then comes to symbolize holistic communication, the elimination of barriers, and the creation of a seamless organization.

Argyris (1990) has discussed the concentrically sealed aspect of both positive and negative communication loops. Once in place, these loops are notoriously difficult to unravel. They are self-reinforcing and resistant to outside intervention. Organization interaction patterns are over determined by these loops, and to change organizations means to effect changes in these loops. That is what OD consultants and other leaders of change do at their best; they help break up vicious circles, sometimes found at the highest levels of leadership, and initiate virtuous circle patterning through all levels of the organization. That is also why consultants who operate from an expert model, alone, might complete good work at the task level of their projects, but are less likely to develop—let alone transform—the organizations they work with. They pay less attention to the cultural and interpersonal residue of both vicious and virtuous circles. These are always present and palpable for those attuned to them, but are capable of being ignored, particularly where projects are highly technical in nature and involve few human beings.

Conversely, where the violation of behavioral expectations is embedded in the organizational culture, the layers of resentment and hostility are often buried deep in the bodies of individuals. If people have stayed for security reasons, as we have sometimes found to be the case, we will often find individuals with deep-seated animosities and resentments, many of whom are in what Peter Bloch (2011) has called a bent-over position from having accommodated themselves to others' needs just once too often!

In systems where people have worked together for years, like the tenure system of academia, it is not unusual for independent, talented professionals to assume they have the right to pursue their own interests, more or less exclusive of the university as a whole. In the first decade of the twenty-first century, with the influx of many contract faculty as part of a new business model for the university, the role of fulltime faculty is once again up for grabs. When the role of fulltime faculty is made the topic of communication between university administration and the fulltime faculty, the gorilla of vicious circles that have existed between the two groups frequently abrogates rational intercourse. Even raising the issue publically may ignite a time bomb of simmering emotions. As a result, meta-communicating about the context of the problem is less likely to succeed than backroom negotiations that involve members of the dominant coalition among faculty, the Dean, and perhaps other power brokers whose presence can serve to equalize the negotiations.

Exceptions aside, systems like this are less likely to serve customers well, nor do they stimulate innovative thinking. There is no such thing as teamwork where mutuality of expectation is missing, and leadership in such a context is daunting. If you have ever heard the phrase, "Watch my back," you will know what I mean. Administrators or faculty who wish to purvey change would do well to enter the fray well armored. We must not assume these are the organizations of the past. Our organizations may be smaller now, with some team practices and a lot of team rhetoric, but they are not necessarily more virtuous.

QUESTIONS FOR SELF-EXPLORATION

1. Consider your work place. What are some of the ways in which you have contributed to the creation of vicious or virtuous circles that may exist there?

2. What specific things might you do to put a stop to one or two of the least vicious communication circles? Is meta-communication an option? Why or why not?

3. What are you doing to initiate and reinforce virtual communication patterns? How do others react to you?

REFERENCES

Block, P. (2011). *Flawless consulting: A guide to getting your expertise used* (3d ed.). San Francisco, CA: Pfeiffer.

Charles Lemart & Ann Branaman (Eds.). (1997). *The Goffman reader.* Malden, MA: Blackwell Publishing.

Rousseau, D. *Psychological contracts in organizations: Understanding written and unwritten agreements.* Thousand Oaks, CA: Sage.

Senge, P. M. (1990) *The fifth discipline: The art & practice of the learning organization.* London, UK: CenturyBusiness.

Watzlawick, P., Beavin, J. H., & Jackson, D. (1967). New York, NY: Norton. *Pragmatics of human communication: A study of interactional patterns, pathologies, and paradoxes.*

LIMITS AND CONTRACTION IN AN AGE OF GROWTH AND EXPANSION

The external forces for change are impersonal and extremely complex. Global competition is an oversimplified explanation of the interplay among multiple initial conditions that have caused and are continuing to fuel the ongoing change revolution. But what if the worst of it has less to do with external factors and more to do with internal ones; the upending going on inside each of us and in our organizations as we try to adapt? Change may have more to do with looking inward, just at the time when the media, the Internet, and our organizations are pushing us to look outward in the competitive, consuming, and entrepreneurial modes. With the economic meltdown and its aftermath, we might want to add the circling the wagons mode to the external and internal focus. We might not be driving our personal and organizational wagons at breakneck speed, right now. Many of us are just trying to stand in place or recover lost ground. It is too soon to say that our society has suddenly gotten religion, seen the error of its ways and had a profound change of heart. Until the results are in, I propose suspending judgment.

My thesis: Human beings have limits, although that is not the popular wisdom of today. Organizations have limits. The way that both individuals and organizations transcend their limits is to first accept them, radically and fully. This is both an inner and an outer journey, and it is not without risk.

The Acceptance of Limits

The promise of our entrepreneurial age is wonderful. Most of us would rather have open-ended opportunities than limitations or constraints. Would it not be nice if the only limitations with which we had to contend were self-imposed? Then we would have some chance of perhaps removing them all! Maybe there are limitless possibilities in the competitive marketplace, but each of them demands a strategy, deploys resources, and evokes consequences, and each of them has a price. In other words, the limits are discovered in the choosing and in the execution of the particular choice that is made. If Company Z enters the Chinese market this year, it probably will have to wait a year or so to enter the European market. If I spend my evenings playing bridge or bar hopping, my children are going to suffer. Life is full of dilemmas and choice points.

Right now there is a lot of novelty and hype in our lives based on the rapid expansion of new technologies on television, on the Internet, and in cellular communications. The economic recession had abridged this but failed to fully deter it. New products and services are constantly invading us. We are told continuously that this is a good thing and that the world can only benefit from this consumer revolution. Like capitalism, the consumers have won! Concepts, theories, and opinions are being wonderfully simplified for us in a brave new world. When space in the brain is limited, the option of careful thought must be eliminated: We have information bits conveyed in nanoseconds, marketing world views transmitted subliminally through hundreds of incomplete sentences and thousands of full-color ads across all forms of media. As Marshall McLuhan implied in a dimly prescient past, "The medium is the message" (2005).

Technology leaders, like the rest of us, would like everyone to buy more and more of what they have to sell. No doubt, ad mavens of the world believe deep within their souls that they are making the world a better place for future generations. Up to a point, with all of this, I have no problem. It is only when the producing and consuming point of view has come to dominate the airwaves and senses and when the ideology of young, wired, and beautiful becomes the dominant ideology that I beg to differ. At this point we have hit an existential wall, beyond which there is a yawning abyss (Barrett 1990)!

It is only the childish mind that assumes always and in every case that there are no limits; the childish mind or the adult mind that does not want to accept limits. If we can only feed the little Cookie Monster within who wants continuous stimulation, we will be truly free (ironically). There must be no abridgement of the rights of the various media and economic interests to continue to create new media and technology that will feed us more and more of what we have come to expect: novelty, innovation, instant satisfaction, dissatisfaction, and more novelty. (We don't necessarily want the dissatisfaction but we get it because it comes with the no limits mindset: Garbage-in—Garbage-out.)

Growth and Limits

We grow by first accepting our limits, not denying them. The manic release of energy occasioned by the collapsing of barriers between countries, cultures, and organizations, the power of the so-called global revolution, has its downside in the generation of technology-driven growth and development misapprehending its own nature. Explosive growth and development is seductive because it does not require individuals to develop a maturity and sense of limits that would help to channel and anchor organization and industry changes. (Surely this is at least partially why we have ended up with the recent global imploding?)

A surer path to grounded success and sustained performance at any level is to expect that any experience of growth and expansion will be periodically punctuated by the experience of deflation and contraction. What goes up must come down. Economists know this, and so does history, but such is our desire to ignore the unpleasant facts of life that we surround ourselves with a **cloud of unknowing** (Anonymous and Underhill 2014). Freud (1938) called this the use of psychological defenses to help us cope with reality. In our day and age, we collectively defend ourselves against seeing the true nature of reality. We allow temporary conditions like bull markets to seduce us into believing that we can continuously engage in risky behavior like buying homes we cannot afford or selling financial derivatives several steps removed from the supposedly secure assets upon which they are based. An entire economy goes into overdrive because relatively complicated economic transactions are simplified so that the average man in the street and corporate interests can be swept up in a wave of growth and prosperity that apparently will never end. We begin to think that buying, selling, production, and profits is the truth and what the whole man is all about. This is the extension of the French philosopher, Voltaire's lampooning of the "best of all possible worlds (2005, 4)" celebrated by the Enlightenment in its worship of science and reason (Barrett 1990). In our recent so-called meltdown, limits were pushed beyond reason to enable capitalism to flourish. One can even distill this from reading popular business magazines, such as Economist and Business Week (2008–2009). Even a right-of-center political and ideological bent cannot easily refute the fact.

Complexity and Limits

The systems interdependence of the global economy is simply the most recent and complex version of a reality full of limits that our societies, and we as individuals, do not wish to face. The controversy over climate change may be another example of this. If we wish to appreciate complexity, before acting as if there were no limits (Vickers 1995), we need to learn that complexity does not respond to oversimplification. When faced with complex dilemmas in our organizations, it is better to turn away from organizational rhetoric, industry pabulum, and the various ministries of propaganda littering our collective landscape to ask

> What is the complete picture here? What does the whole situation, past, present, and future, look like? What are the critical issues that must be addressed, the key decisions to be made? What is a reasonable outcome in this situation? What do I need to do to effect that outcome? What is my gut telling me? What does my rational mind have to contribute?

Individually and organizationally, we frequently face complexity. Unfortunately, our all-pervasive age of speed and simplification has led us to apply the techniques of the marketplace to the problems of the workplace. And this had led us to deny and mistrust our own experience. To that extent, we do not know who we are anymore.

The Importance of Turning Inward

Women who have borne children, at least during the period of pregnancy, are pulled deeply into what is happening inside them. Most learn to trust the experience of life developing within (author's opinion generalizing from multiple discussions and participant observation). One might say that women are anchored in what psychoanalyst Erik Erikson conceives of as an **inner space** (2001). Conversely, Western culture—gender emancipation notwithstanding—is arguably male dominated and conceives of this space as a dark inner jungle where a man might lose his way and quite literally be castrated by the power of the feminine. (Allow me some liberty with Freudian Theory. Business ideology, norms, and assumptions will deny this and yet, as a counseling psychologist, I take my stand.) The male's natural thrusting force becomes limp in the face of this dark, putatively aggressive unknown power. Men in our culture are taught to externalize their experience, projecting it on to the outside world, testing it against common sense and the collec1tive wisdom, and obsessively measuring against so-called objective criteria. (Profits, ROI, Quarterly Returns, Season Statistics). If women have access to an inner space, we might hope for an alternative to the all-pervasive market economy worldview coming from their quarter. That would be a false hope. In today's world, all of us, both men and women, are lopsided externalizers (Berger and Luckmann 1967). Externalizer dominance is a cultural fact. It occurs in most of our organizations, with perhaps the exception of those that measure success as a change in the inner life of their clients. Churches and counseling centers, for example, point their customers inward to reconnect with their own personal and spiritual cores. Trusting in your own experience rather than in the multiple and massive meanings that have come to invade our minds, means that we must first learn how to *fully experience*. This means balancing the external focus of our business culture with an inner space orientation. External is speeding up, capturing market share, or reducing cycle time. Internal is slowing down, connecting with one's inner power and grace, or growing an organizational culture of rich possibilities. In our national culture, unfortunately, and somewhat paradoxically, focusing inward is often perceived as navel-gazing.

Ironically, one of our most introverted activities seems to be continuously checking our cell phones in order to network with others on social media. We look away from others who are right by our side to link-in with online friends whose faces tell us little about what could be communicated through the immediacy of their presence. We present ourselves on the Web in ways that invoke either impression management or global neighborhood picnics. The dichotomy between internal and external/introversion and extroversion has broken down (Jung 1976). We are all either learning to be more complete communicators or communication itself has lost some of its meaning[1].

If we are to flourish in the midst of complex change, we must learn to trust our experience. In the face of global change this means that we must spend at least part of our time focusing inward and gaining access to a spiritual center. The spiritual center is not just a brain, a body, and a belief system that evokes self-transcendence. It is a place where all three overlap and interconnect. It is who we really are beyond the face and role we present to others. If we do not learn to trust our full experience, in the sense I am describing here, the strongest executive becomes weak in the face of global or industry dynamics that do not respond to externalizing, manipulating, controlling, or grasping behavior. Alternatively, the most powerful and graceful executives become ineffective if they cannot integrate these same attributes of inwardness with creative externalizing skills. In an age of change and discontinuity we ourselves must change, and change deeply.[2]

---

1   I push this example to make a point. I'm an avid fan of Linkedin. I use it for both marketing and impression management purposes. I love the friends who I make there!

2   Interestingly, in the year of this book's publication, 2016, the world has been sobered by limits: Wars that cannot be won in the Middle East, hungry children in inner cities juxtaposed to stocked granaries in the Midwest, Syrian refugee camps in a bewildered Europe.

DISCUSSION QUESTIONS FOR SELF-EXPLORATION

1. Can you see patterns of expansion and risk-taking balanced against limits and contractions in your own career?

2. What can individuals and organizations do to cultivate an inner space orientation?

3. How can you as a manager keep things under control without becoming overly obsessed with control?

REFERENCES

Anonymous, & Underhill. (2014). *The cloud of unknowing.* (Digitally Delivered. Retrieved from https://www.amazon.com/gp/digital/fiona)

Barrett, W. (1990). *Irrational man.* New York, NY: Anchor Books.

Berger, P. L., & Luckmann, T. (1967). *The social construction of reality.* New York, NY: Anchor Press.

Jung, C. (1976) *The portable Jung.* New York, NY: Penguin Classics.

McLuhan, M. & Fiore, Q. (2005). *The medium is the message.* Berkeley, CA: Gingko Press.

Robert Coles (Ed.). (2001). *The Erik Erikson reader.* New York, NY: Norton.

Vickers, G. (1995). *The art of judgment: A study of policy making.* Thousand Oaks, CA: Sage.

Voltaire, F. (2005/1801). *Candide: Or optimism.* New York, NY: Penguin Classics.

*Economist and Bloomberg Businessweek.

A Shift of Mindset

In the last decade of the twentieth century, Peter Senge (1993), an M.I.T. management thinker, and two notable professors of organizational behavior, Chris Argyris and Donald Schön (1996), popularized a topic from management research which has been available in the management literature for forty-five years (Argyris 1967; Cangelosi and Dill 1965). It is called organizational learning. Senge and his associates did some research with progressive and innovative companies and uncovered strategies and insights essential to the creation of flexible, adaptive organizations. His basic premise was that organizations needed to be capable of learning in order to adjust to the long-term hurricane conditions we face today. For Senge, learning was not just assimilating new information or even developing new competencies. Learning entailed a basic shift in the way we see and think about our worlds. If individuals and organizations were learning, it meant that they were increasing their abilities to continuously create and recreate their own futures (13–14).

Most societies have recognized that learning is important for individuals. In this country, if we can afford it, we put our children in pre-school, drive them in the pursuit of academic excellence from then on, and hope they have internalized enough concepts and skills to make their way in this world. It is only within the last fifteen years that learning has become a hot topic for organizations (Senge, 1996). In truth, corporate entities of the past could get away with very little of the type of learning we discuss in this chapter. Protective markets,

Previously published in *Journal of Management and Marketing Research*, vol. 9, March 2012. Article Copyright © 2012 by Jeff Haldeman.

lack of meaningful competition, and the supremacy of command-and-control structures reduced the need for organizational learning. The task environments of most organizations were in low gear. Organizations could function, even succeed, without developing much. Most of them did. Learning and development has now become important to organizations because they are exposed to the rapid movement of capital, customers, and societies in ways that threaten existence. There has been a global shift, and the 2007–2010 global recession notwithstanding, all sectors of the economy will continue to adjust to and capitalize on this shift.

What this author means by a learning organization is a group of people, large or small, who are organized to produce specific products or services. They are bounded off from other groups and constantly engaged in an ongoing process of (1) focusing on their environment to collect data on stakeholder expectations, (2) realigning structures, systems, and processes to respond to change, and (3) continually confronting dysfunctions which threaten to impede organization effectiveness leadership, team work, and customer satisfaction (Cawsey and Deszca, 2012). Put another way, the learning organization recognizes that the environment is constantly changing and changes itself to keep pace with these external shifts. Individuals and teams must learn together or risk dysfunction. This is an ironclad rule. The author's premise is that all organizations that fail to learn will become dysfunctional on some level. Organizations that are dysfunctional will fail to recognize or adapt to significant changes in their environments. While they may or may not survive as an organization, once dysfunctional dynamics are entrenched, the path back to learning is both a painful—and occasionally exhilarating—process. It requires sustained commitment and courage. Like individuals, most organizations would rather procrastinate than change.

I will illustrate both the power and pain of organizational learning by presenting a case example of an organization I consulted to for three years. It started out as a product of mergers and acquisitions. Several traditional transit agencies merged to form this new entity, Tranzex (not its real name). Located close to a dynamic and expanding urban center, the agency found itself quickly pressed to expand services to accommodate a diverse and differentiated customer base. Born as a new entity, it still possessed the cultural artifacts and baggage of the smaller agencies from which it was formed. The public transportation industry is heavily regulated and answerable to many stakeholder groups and constituencies. This means many rules and procedures, the bureaucracy that inevitably accompanies regulation.

I will (1) describe the background of the organization, (2) illustrate how it was characterized by numerous learning disabilities (Senge 1993, 17–18), and (3) show how Senge's Laws of the Fifth Discipline (57–58) kept the organization from escaping its plight. Next, I will describe how a process of organization development was used to engage all employees in the difficult process of learning how to learn.

A Case Example

This organization was located in the Pacific Northwest and was about twenty years old. For most of its short life, it had known only passivity and insulation in the management ranks. In the previous ten years, management had introduced a variety of change programs each of which lost momentum as money and long-term leadership failed to materialize. These were consultant-centered projects with management taking the lead in giving lip service to consultant initiatives. Participative management was a buzzword. There was very little effective management occurring, period. The question of participation was moot.

Tranzex had had two management audits done during the five years prior to this consultant's involvement. Both had said that internal communications and management practices needed to be fixed. The board of directors (hereafter, the board) had carefully noted the results of these audits and also become aware that the deepest source of their worries lay in an executive team that was failing to provide leadership. Tranzex had plenty of slack resources. Unlike many area organizations, Tranzex could afford to spend money to begin turning itself around. Access to funds proved to be a two-edged sword. Again and again, management called in consultants to make change. Each time the organization's culture spit them out. Eventually, the members of the organization had little hope that anything would ever change. The board itself had gotten into the habit of micromanaging to compensate for the mistakes of executive management. Over time, it became clear to the board that something new was required to break the organizational impasse.

The new thing turned out to be major changes in the organization's external world: Tranzex was part of a rapidly growing metropolitan region that was calling for more and diverse consumer offerings. What was once a sleepy county punctuated by a major interstate artery had become a bustling center for urban transportation. The prospect of regionalization and consolidation of services had emerged as a threat to the agency's autonomy.

As demands for service exploded, the old executive team struggled to keep up; a longer-term paralysis was deepening within the organizational system. The Board was forced to take drastic measures.

In summary, for this consultant, Tranzex was a prototype and challenge for leading change. It faced what many organizations steeped in the old ways have had to face: Lack of leadership, ineffective structures for teamwork, strained employee relations, management training disconnected from strategy, and communication walls between departments. Disrespect for authority was rampant, top-down. On the plus side, it was equally well–endowed: A board convinced of the need for radical change, a creative and committed work force that cared deeply about serving customers, and a fairly secure funding base.

Barriers to Learning

Tranzex had many of the barriers to learning that often accompany traditional work systems:

1. Narrowly defined jobs and decision powers coupled with too much autonomy. The employees were always falling over each other in an attempt to get the job done with little supervision to help them find their way. (Counterintuitively, too little supervision is often worse than micro-management in a culture of executive indifference. A management and leadership vacuum existed which failed to link the operating core of the organization with broader strategic purposes.)

2. No meaningful feedback loops for learning. The performance management system was outdated and irrelevant, a relic of an earlier area in industrial relations. Across the board, employees simply were not accountable for their performance, and people did not know where they stood. There was no meaningful dialogue or work-related conversation across levels or functions.

3. Throughout the organization there was lack of information flow. The top had effectively conditioned everyone else to stop asking questions. Years before, they had buried their heads in the sand.

4. There were system barriers and delays as typified by an incredibly long and un-wieldy purchasing process with numerous non-value-added steps.

5. First-line supervision was unionized and seen as stubborn, rule oriented, and authoritarian. They lacked mental models or personal visions for being anything else. In the absence of changes to the larger organizational system, periodic management training had little impact.

6. A culture of self-protection and divisiveness had become part of the warp and woof of the organization.

7. Cooperation was modeled mostly in emergencies when the dysfunctional community members came together against an outside enemy.

8. Few work groups performed like teams, so most did not know what teamwork was supposed to look like. In the absence of appropriate models or team designs (Thompson 2007), workers created what they knew and had previously experienced: Under-organized (Brown 1989) interest groups who rarely supported the goals of the organization.

9. There had been a fair amount of problem solving activity, but few solutions had been implemented. As a result, there was a deep cynicism about the link between action and results. This is sometimes known as the activity theory of organization effectiveness. Activity and passivity alternate but neither is tied to performance improvement or results.

10. Work groups were fragmented and dominated by difficult people (Bramson 1981). Fortunately, small prototypes for teamwork existed in enclaves throughout the organization. The people involved tended to cling to these centers of excellence and resist contamination by the larger culture and work system.

11. There were norms of management by committee alongside a culture of management abdication. The essence of the bargain was this: "We managers cannot or will not make essential decisions, so you, our committees, are free to decide what we have never given you the power, authority, or resources to decide. You will pretend to do your work, and we will pretend to sanction your efforts. Everyone will be frustrated, but no one will talk about it openly or admit any personal accountability for the process and outcomes." In diagnostic assessments, the consultants found a proliferation of employee committees, offering the promise of employee involvement and never getting beyond brainstorming.

12. Conflict avoidance was the norm. There were supervisory and employee unions, but because there were plenty of resources to go around and pay was good, a culture of collusion had evolved. In layman's terms: "You scratch my back, and I'll scratch yours." There was too little conflict to generate a meaningful and constructive devil's advocate role for the unions. The organization lacked boundaries; nor did it have the structures, systems, and processes to constructively channel the heat of differences. People colluded in agreeing not to face very real differences and interests. Top management led the way.

13. In the absence of effective leadership, blaming and self-protection ran rampant.

To summarize, the system had been held in place by mutually reinforcing negative feedback loops, a rule-oriented compliance culture, and management rejection of facts and opinions that challenged the reality they had collectively created. More importantly, they lacked a holistic framework for understanding the impact of structures, forces, and processes within the organizational system.

Countercultural Values and Other Assets

To provide grounds for hope, one needed to look beyond the learning challenges to uncover countercultural values that contradicted the dominant management ideology. One might call these the values of both the subversive real and ideal organizations. Their presence pointed the way to a shared future of organizational integrity and excellence:

1. In spite of everything, many employees strongly believed that Tranzex had the potential to be a leader in transportation.

2. Employees were highly educated and strong on customer service. They tended to personify the interest in the new and innovative that characterized this part of the country.

3. Many employees had incipient personal visions ready to be tapped if only management had the will to do so.

4. A small cadre of employees was dedicated to personal mastery (Senge 1993, 7–8) for the higher purpose of making Tranzex a better place to work. Role models from the bottom, they were reinforced by elements of the informal system and sustained by their own sense of values and purpose.

5. Some union leaders and middle management had been counter cultural. Their strategy was "Be pleasant, persistent, and active. Continue to push for results. Be satisfied with small steps." This is what social psychologist Debra Meyerson might call a tempered radical (2001).

How Consultants Can Mess Things Up

Simplistic consultant solutions do not address the full complexity of the organization-in-its-situation. Consequently, consultants who rely on one-trick pony action plans will come up short. Here is my analysis when applied to Tranzex:

1. Periodic infusions of consultant-led change activity gives false hope. Management acts as if they are doing something significant; plans are made, action steps proffered, enthusiasm generated. The situation gets better before it gets worse (57). This happens each time a new consultant is brought in (albeit on a curve of decreasing magnitude). We all want to believe that things can change for the better, and we frequently undermine our own best judgments that it just is not so.

2. Simple solutions to complex problems do not work (58). All previous change-related activities were short-lived and things returned to normal fairly quickly.

3. Consultants don't heal organizations; organizations must heal from within (61). Bringing in consultants became a bad habit that used up organizational resources, staff commitment, and work hours. Managers never really acted on their recommendations, at least not in a timely way. As Senge notes, the organization becomes dependent on single-note, addictive solutions, which generates one-size-fits-all mentalities. This is worse than doing nothing: The practice will actually speed the deterioration of the organization.

4. Modeling the reasons for the status quo is difficult. Cause and effect relationships are often blurred (63). This was augmented by a learned helplessness (Yen 1998) phenomenon at Tranzex, which asked the question, "Why even try?" Lack of motivation, models, and roadmaps for change collectively led to an inability to learn or change. Managers and employees were unable to see that outmoded structures, systems, and management practices were at the heart of the organization's problem. They had become blind to the growing mismatch between external demands and organization's ability to respond.

5. Being busy, we all want the most impact for the least effort (63). The question is, What organizational elements can you leverage to produce that? The answer, in this organization, was not to introduce a series of programs with a lot of hoopla. That looks like change but is not. As anyone who has achieved a surprising result may know, just pulling the right group of people together, with a clear focus, in a quiet, low-key way, will often produce better outcomes.

6. Blaming managers and employees for the current state might be a fruitless endeavor (67). That is not to say that people should not be held accountable, but blame is something different. As long as there is blame, there tends not to be meaningful action and results. Under blame conditions, employees cannot and will not act in concert to accomplish goals or solve problems. The organization gets caught in its own trap. Everyone has a reason for not acting and the more we try to avoid getting blamed, the more we are likely to blame others and ourselves. We should know by now, blame contracts and constricts, responsibility and accountability expands and enlivens!

One Organization's Path Back to Sanity

Change finally came to this organization, and it did appear to have happened gradually. Years of unresponsive management finally combined with (1) external stakeholder criticism, (2) rapid growth of potential ridership, (3) the cumulative impact of consultant studies, and (4) board weariness to bring Tranzex to the point of impasse. They simply had to act, finally, at a broad systems level with a systems understanding; no more piecemeal efforts to dislodge the problem. It was time to move from vicious to virtuous circles (Senge 1993: 81–83). As any good student of change knows, no dysfunctional system bound up in vicious circles can change itself, by itself, from within (Watzlawick, Weakland, and Fisch 1974). In this case, the solutions were fairly straightforward, if not easy to implement. They all supported and required a primary change objective of learning how to learn. These steps represent what was actually accomplished at Tranzex. We present them as recommendations because we know from experience that they work:

Recommendation 1: Replace the old senior managers with a new executive director and senior management team. Seed the organization with strong leadership and use qualified internal and external change consultants to help identify leverage points for system change that could be acted upon in a sustained way.

Recommendation 2: Create a shared vision that is driven from the top and grounded in reality, not just a wish-list. Avoid platitudes and promises that are devoid of meaning for stakeholder groups. Include members of all stakeholder groups to help shape it.

Recommendation 3: Build an integrated, sequenced plan for strategic change that flows directly from assessments of the organization's current culture and management structure. This plan should be developed and driven by the executive team, with full Board support.

Recommendation 4: Coach key executives in vision derived behaviors and role modeling. These new role models will determine success as they go about the day-to-day task of aligning the organization with a shared vision and strategic objectives. For a long time, they will be the primary vision bearers that everyone else will look to for confirmation that change is occurring.

Recommendation 5: Ensure that the board and executive team agree on proposed changes and that the employee vision for change is given focus and voice.

Recommendation 6: Conceptualize and communicate change as an ongoing and never-ending process. Specific change programs and OD interventions end. The process of organizational transformation, learning, and adaptation does not.

Recommendation 7: Move the implementation of this plan down, into, and across the organization by creating a series of prototype team learning situations.

  » At Tranzex, the executive team, board, and a diagonal slice of fifteen people from across the organization created the first draft of the shared vision.
  » A Maintenance Department task team developed standards and procedures for bus mechanics. The process itself of enacting the change created teamwork.
  » A communications team chartered by management redesigned the operations department and implemented the new team based design.

Recommendation 8: Educate everyone in the organization on the shared vision. Be open and truthful about the past. There is no point in hiding what we all know. It will be refreshing to have stakeholders build a path to the future by standing on solid ground. Dysfunctional organizations are built upon lies and misperceptions. Expose the lies. Challenge the misperceptions and declare victory over them. Then clean-up the organization as you go forward.

Recommendation 9: Be honest about what it will take to really change the way we operate and do business. It will take time, money, training, coaching, and leadership. It will take an executive team that leads the charge and sustains momentum over years. They will put their own values and behaviors on the line, explicitly. They will ask all stakeholder groups to do the same. Effective leadership will diffuse into all parts of the organization. The plan is to hold each other accountable.

Recommendation 10: Once you, as leaders, have established your credibility, do not tolerate role models or behaviors that clearly express an allegiance to the old ways of management and organization. Many have felt Jack Welch's management policies at GE had a draconian flavor (Welch 2005, 37–51). Each year, the bottom ten percent of managers, those who were clearly not performing in line with vision and strategy, were fired. Whether you agree with him or not, he did a number of things right: (1) As CEO, he created mission and strategy at the executive level, (2) he had the rest of the organization help develop the vision and values they would live by, (3) he provided his executives and managers with all the tools, training, and coaching they would need to change behavior, (4) he gave them some time to develop, and (5) he held them accountable. Jack supported performers but did not coddle non-performers. He poured extensive resources into individual and organizational learning, and then said, "Show me that you have learned something that will make a significant contribution to this organization." That is what leadership, management, and organizational citizenship are all about.

Principles of Effective Change Leadership

It is tempting to get even more specific about all of the exciting changes that were introduced into this organization. However, only a few basic principles were leveraged, and these were the keys to our success in creating a learning organization:

1. Tranzex expanded learning and development (T&D) to cover the entire organization. This included fundamental, behaviorally focused coaching and group process skills training for executives, managers and supervisors. Tranzex also implemented 360° feedback and development with key executives.

2. Critical leadership behaviors were embedded in the performance plans of all managers. Managers were trained to competency in these behaviors, and held accountable for results. The process started with the senior leadership team.

3. Management, not consultants, led the change effort. The executive team accepted employee skepticism and distrust and countered it with openness, a results-focus, and a refusal to be intimidated by failures or mistakes. All this is at the heart of organizational learning.

4. Tranzex focused on strengthening the basic integrity of leadership and management before looking to partner with the three unions in some sort of formal power sharing agreement. The unions supported change, in principle, but in the beginning were not ready to put their own integrity on the line. Years of working in collusion with previous leadership had created a cozy status quo. They both did and did not want to rock the boat. No matter. Focused results, employee involvement in the shared vision process, and momentum generated by executive leadership eventually got the unions more interested. When a labor-management steering committee was finally formed, it was created on the basis of management results already achieved.

5. The consultant(s) contracted and interacted with all levels of the organization. They were not overly reliant on leveraging the power of the top.

6. Client organization commitment to a structured, multi-year change effort ensured that organizational learning would have time to diffuse throughout the system. After the first year, change momentum was powerful enough so that more people had to take a stand in relation to the change leaders and to the process and outcomes of change itself. Core systems, structures, and relationships had changed, and leadership had kept its promises. There were fewer and fewer places to hide.

7. Tranzex completed a restructuring of the management ranks to ensure that managers who had not been and were not currently pulling their weight would be held accountable. They were replaced, as necessary. Many of these terminations occurred during the first year of the change effort. This was unusual for the industry and sent the message to the rank and file that managers were at long last expected to lead and manage. Not all change efforts require massive restructuring (reengineering), but change leaders must be willing to remove roadblocks and non-performers. Otherwise, and in a very real sense, preservation of the status quo will triumph over goals for fundamental change.

DISCUSSION QUESTIONS FOR SELF-EXPLORATION

1. Using the case example as a guide, identify at least three barriers to organization learning in your work unit or organization.

2. Assess your own work group around these dysfunctions. (Use a 1–7 rating scale, 1= "Not at all characteristic," 7 = "Very characteristic.")

3. In each case, explain how you either attempted to overcome the Learning challenge or contributed to it.

REFERENCES

Argyris, C. (1967). Today's problems with tomorrow's organizations. *Journal of Management Studies, 4*(1), 31–55.

Argyris, C. & Schön, D. A. (1996). *Organizational learning II: Theory, method, and practice.* Reading, MA: Addison-Wesley.

Bramson, R. M. (1981). *Coping with difficult people.* New York, NY: Anchor Press.

Brown, L. D. (1989). Research action in many worlds [White paper]. Retrieved from http://www.scu.edu.au/schools/gcm/ar/w/LDavidBrown.pdf

Cangelosi, V. E., & Dill, W. R. (1965). Organizational learning: observations toward a theory. *Administrative Science Quarterly, 10,* 175–203.

Senge, P. M. (1993). *The fifth discipline: The art and practice of the learning organization.* London, England: Century Business.

Thompson, L. L. (2008) *Making the team* (3rd ed.). Upper Saddle River, NJ: Pearson.

Watzlawick, P., Weakland, J. H., Fisch, R. (1974). *Change: Principles of problem formation and problem resolution.* New York, NY: W. W. Norton.

Welch, J. (2005). *Winning.* New York, NY: Harper Business.

Yen, D. H. (1998). Learned helplessness. Retrieved from http://www.noogenesis.com/malama/discouragement/helplessness.html

THE MORAL MANAGER IN A GLOBAL CONTEXT

A Historical Requiem

Rabid anti-Semitism—fear and hatred of the Jewish people—was endemic to Germany and to other parts of Europe well before the Nazis ever came to power. Author Hannah Arendt (2003) has written extensively about this and noted that dehumanizing conditions did not emerge from a cultural vacuum or as an artifact of the horrors of war. To understand the cultural context is to understand many of the questions and answers about how violence, in its various forms, can flourish in a supposedly civilized society.

Big Data and Big Violence

We treat these facts as ancient history, no longer relevant to our Knowledge Age. Strangely enough, here in our own world, global context is producing a potentially dehumanizing aspect that is affecting a broad spectrum of international regions, nations, peoples, and organizations. On the positive side, there are global flows of knowledge, products, and services that benefit many nations and regions. On the negative side, these flows are frequently disrupted by wars of aggression, terrorism, counter-terrorism, economic sanctions against aggressor nations, and cyber-attacks.

In the United States, we have finally recovered from the 2007 global recession. We have supply chain economics, big data analytics, and master's programs in cyber security. We have the reality of global partnerships and partnerships within industrial sectors. Merger mania had a strong year in 2015[1]. There is global collaboration and progress in the business sector, because there the bottom line is clear. In the West we have democracy and infrastructure to support our business and entrepreneurial efforts. The corporate sector will do what it needs to maintain profits and sustain longer-term growth. Is this a return to a business and economic stability that will benefit us all? Broader evidence might be implying, no. Geopolitical forces are buffeting our societies and our organizations. The Eurozone is struggling to assimilate refugees from North Africa and Syria[2]. Globally, there are trends such as climate change, and cultural and governmental upheavals in the Middle East. Russia has reappeared in the guise of a rogue nation, and ISIS, Boko Haram, and other terrorist groups are committing mass murders on an accelerating basis. Terrorist fingerprints have been in the United States since at least September 11, 2001. The year 2015 saw many violent attacks on schools, organizations, and people in this country. On average, **four or more people were left wounded or dead every day** of the year[3].

Geopolitical Contexts and Organizational Behavior

In this chapter, I will review our current geopolitical context and argue that this context, composed of both progressive and inhumane elements,

1   Porzio, M. 2015, October. "Is Record M&A Activity Sustainable?" *Forbes.* Retrieved from http://forbes.com

2   Nuttall, T. (2015, November). "The Migrant Mess." *The Economist, The World in 2016*, 95.

3   LaFraniere, S., Cohen, S., & Oppel, R. A., Jr. "How Often Do Mass Shootings Occur? On Average, Every Day. Records Show." http://www.nytimes.com/2015/12/03/us/how-often-do-mass-shootings-occur-on-average-every-day-records-show.html?_r=0 (2 Dec. 2015)

can begin to create conditions and forces, which, left unchecked, could lead to dehumanizing behaviors in many organizations. We in America enjoy relative stability compared to the rest of the world. We are not used to periods of protracted turbulence, uncertainty, and economic decline. We have now entered a brand new era of global prosperity, global inequity, and global violence. Because of electronic media, men and women everywhere know about it. It is unclear how our nation and our organizations will fare. There are implications for executives, managers, and employees in all of our organizations.

We will ask: (1) What happens at the intersection between organizations and their geopolitical contexts? (2) Are there forces now operating in organizations that produce both performance and dehumanization? (3) How will you recognize the dehumanizing elements of organization when you are experiencing them? (4) What is the courageous and honorable way to behave when you feel trapped in a dehumanizing organization?

The Context for Dehumanization

In Guantanamo Bay, Cuba, post-9/11 terrorist suspects were held for interrogation and treated in a way that looked suspiciously like torture[4]. The discrepancy between our national disavowal of torture and evidence that water-boarding had been used to interrogate enemy combatants and suspected Al Qaeda leaders led President Barack Obama to sign a presidential order in 2009 to close the prison down[5].

As the Zimbardo (2007) research demonstrates, when the right conditions are created, people will engage in behaviors of which they had previously thought themselves incapable. This occurs irrespective of nation, race, creed, gender, or ethnicity. In the Zimbardo research, young men in a university course designed to simulate the effects of prison conditions easily fell into their roles: Student guards harassed student prisoners, and student prisoners becoming passive and depressed. They were not directed to do this; they did it automatically. This simulation was a two-week research project that had to be called off after six days due to the traumatic impact on the students, and perhaps on Zimbardo, himself.

Reflecting back thirty years later, Zimbardo admitted that as the warden of the prison, he had fallen into "passivity in allowing the abuses to continue as long as I did—an evil of inaction" (2004). His initial underestimation of the power of oppressive organizations to shape behavior helped spark a long-term research interest that later culminated in a book, *The Lucifer Effect* (2004). This work chronicled the abuse perpetrated by U.S. Army prison guards at the Abu Graib facility in Afghanistan.

There is then a precedent for suggesting that Western democracies like the United States are vulnerable to the forces of violence and extremism. The enslavement of African-Americans in the American South and both the massacre and movement onto reservations of the American Indian are two other notable examples. I mention these not to show that even the best of nations are imperfect but to show that even terms like best nation may be held suspect when measured against the right moral calculus.

---

4 Finn and Warrick, March 9, 2009
5 Trans. January 22, 2009

Organization as an Ideal Type

To facilitate this analysis, I will use sociologist Max Weber's methodological device of the **ideal type**[6] to transmit some truths about organization. An ideal type is an extreme, purer form of organization abstracted from the elements of countless real-life, concrete organizations. Weber wrote about bureaucracy as an ideal type composed of certain essential elements and attributes that probably no single organization of his time completely possessed (1978). His focus was on hierarchy, rules, and personnel selection based on merit as forms of organizational design suitable for the rational (read ideal) organization. He believed in the efficiency and effectiveness of bureaucracy. Few organizations of his day achieved his criteria for the bureaucratic ideal type, yet he was able to get at certain essentials of organizational effectiveness that pointed the way to the organization of the future. Over time, bureaucracy became the dominant organizational form. In the late twentieth and early twenty-first centuries, Fortune 500 companies were practically all bureaucracies, or modern counterparts thereof, the corporate divisionalized structure. Managers would do well to remember that though we often speak of bureaucracies and bureaucrats with disdain, the shift to that organizational form corrected many of the worst excesses of nepotism and corruption that existed in earlier organizational forms.

On the Road to Ferguson

In the United States, urban police departments serving multi-racial neighborhoods might be considered a **negative ideal type**, crystallizing certain negative aspects of a service organization whose norms have been perverted in the name of safety and justice. Having lived five miles away from Ferguson, MO, for the last nine years, the author cannot help but draw parallels between the killing of Michael Brown, the violent norms toward African-Americans that apparently existed within the police department, and the context of racial discrimination that the facts of the case support[7]. Both government reports and news investigations provided the evidence that systematic racial bias and profiling was a part of that police department's way of doing business. Poor African-Americans were fined for minor traffic violations, put in prison because they could not afford to pay, and in certain cases, were left there to languish. To top it off, a city with a majority black population had a police force that was predominately white[8]. How does this happen in a supposedly democratic nation with a relatively humane legal system? As additional evidence of the racially motivated animosities between big city police forces and African-American citizens continued to mount through 2015, we began to see, once again, that ghetto-like conditions had persisted in our inner cities for decades after Martin Luther King, Malcolm X, and the Freedom Riders. The Rodney King case in 1992, in Los Angeles, California, is another example of police violence

---

6   Stanford Encyclopedia of Philosophy, 2007, Section 5.2

7   Appuzo, M. (2015). Ferguson police routinely violate rights of blacks, Justice Depart. finds. *The New York Times*, http://www.nytimes.com/2015/03/04/us/justice-department-finds-pattern-of-police-bias-excessive-force-in-ferguson.html?_r=0.

8   Appuzo, M., & Eligon, J. (2015). Ferguson police tainted by bias, Justice Department says. http://www.nytimes.com/2015/03/05/us/us-calls-on-ferguson-to-overhaul-criminal-justice-system.html

in economically deprived areas that are devoid of resources[9]. Under such conditions, accompanied by real and imagined fears of the populations they are supposed to protect, police departments have the potential for becoming like the guards in the Zimbardo experiments. Nazi Germany restricted Jewish people to ghettos and racial profiling. Why should we be surprised that dehumanization is not just the stepchild of war or individual cretins who just happen to have found their way into our police departments?

High Involvement and the Piggy Phenomenon (Golding 2011)

In 2016, it is fashionable to laud the entrepreneurial high-involvement organization as our organization of the future, an ideal type characterized by teamwork, participative management, customer focus, and relentless, time-based competition (Cummings and Worley 2009, 367–372). The entrepreneurial organization is downsized, geared to flexibility of response, and supposedly invested in employee commitment. In an environment characterized by global competition, however, the military metaphors of strategy and tactics are still in use in many organizations. Without stretching, some managers may even believe that brutal competition calls for a take-no-prisoners leadership and management style. There is a perverse logic to it: "We cannot waste time tolerating weak performance or performers. In the face of constant change and its stresses, we have to get people in line!" We no longer seem to have the time to develop people. With the loss of job security in many organizations, we expect people to be glad they have a job, and maybe, to shut up and be glad they have a job. We don't say this out loud to employees; we usually just imply it, reinforced by a leveraged managerial scowl. Executives are not above withdrawing access as a form of pressure to conform.

Interestingly, evidence has shown that high involvement work systems have such strong performance-based norms that they will scapegoat individuals who, for one reason or another, no longer seem to be making the grade (Burke 1969). It is the teams that are not well developed or skilled in performance management who are particularly prone to attack individuals in the face of severe work pressures. The high levels of cooperation required to get the job done may lead to a certain intolerance of individuals who seem to be a drag on the team. Everyone may know what's wrong, but no one wants to take the lead to confront it. If the teams are self-managed, it requires a strong, well-trained team manager to step in and either hold the team accountable or take action themselves (Thompson 2010). Enough managers lack these high level team skills and sensitivities that we often find a team is one in name only. With a poor team design, lack of training, and poor leadership or sponsorship from the next level, a work team that remains intact often becomes a disaffected group. Over time, it may become something like a low-level, disorganized mob—angry, depressed, and dysfunctional. Groups like this may develop norms of low performance and bully new team members into suppressing their initial excitement and desire to perform.

There is also evidence that many organizations have only partially incorporated the self-managed team concept and redesign into what was previously a bureaucratic work system

---

9 Mydans, S. (1992). The police verdict; Los Angelas policeman acquited in taped beating. *The New York Times*. Retrieved from https://www.nytimes.com/books/98/02/08/home/rodney-verdict.html

(Haldeman 1991). When this happens, a hybrid gets created with all the worst elements of bureaucracy standing side-by-side with models of team effectiveness that are only partially realized. An organization design like this, ill- suited to its purposes, is likely to lead to internal pressures, dysfunction, and abusive behaviors and communication, within and without the self-managed teams (Haldeman 1991).

To Get to Ideal, Let's Be Real

There may have been a sea change from hierarchical command-and-control to team-based self-management, but where exactly is the evidence? There are, of course, organizational exemplars such as those mentioned in *Good to Great* (Collins 2001). These companies are noted for their humane, energizing work environments, their inspiring visions of service and success, and the impressive bottom-line results they have achieved. Companies like this clearly do exist, but one could argue that they are not in the majority. On the other hand, unenlightened managers are unlikely to invite management consultants or academic researchers in to describe or theorize about that lack of enlightenment. So, the popular business press tends to paint pictures of success (Collins and Porras 2004). This sells books, and heaven forbid that we should be negative. It's not good for the brand. This author would agree that modeling our organizations after exemplars can take us a certain distance. It is inspiring. It is motivating. We want to close the gap. As managers, we are action-oriented and required to make innumerable quick decisions every day (Mintzberg 2005). We can hardly afford much time for reflection or second-guessing of ourselves. That being the case, we will want to be confident about the way we manage people and to believe we are doing as well as anyone could! We all want to believe the best about ourselves (Taylor 1989). Yet, as managers we would do well to also be sensitized to models of dysfunction and failure as well as to models of organization effectiveness and transformation. It is easy to delude oneself into thinking that one's management style and workplace is at the forefront of progress. In the absence of third-party evidence, who is to say differently?

We have an entrepreneurial revolution touted by management bestsellers (Hamel 2002) alongside real managers who are too busy selling, managing their organizations, and running their numbers to trouble themselves much with human resource practices or questions. This is not ideally the way they might want it to be. This is the way it is.

How We End-up Treating People Like Objects

Pressure is put on employees in downsized organizations today where people are expected to do more and more with less and less. I will show how this can lead to a tendency to objectify people, to see them as pieces to be moved around on the chess table of strategy and operations. People are exploited as objects in a global war of competition.

Language as Desensitizer

Most of our organizations are open systems (Katz and Kahn 1998). They are responsive to expectations and feedback from customers and other stakeholders, which cause them to modify their products, practices, and services. There is also, of course, our legal system, originally based upon English common law and reflecting the moralistic premises of a relatively just and humane society. However, just because an organization is more of an open system and laws restrict the most aberrant human relations abuses does not mean that management practices are necessarily humanistic or progressive. Today, when we speak about organizations, dysfunctional or not, we use everyday language to describe them. To illustrate the point, let us take the example of the open systems model used by management and behavioral scientists to explain how normal organizations operate (Katz and Kahn 1998). In an organizational open system, product or service inputs are (1) combined with money, materials, and other resources, and then (2) transformed by a technical work process (the work methods and technologies which transform the raw materials). When these methods or tools are (3) applied to the various raw material inputs by the organization's human operators, and this is done in a specified and consistent manner, (4) a finished product or service is created, which is passed on to a customer for use. In an ideal world, the customer either buys the product or not, and is satisfied or not. The customer response is supposed to eventually be tallied and fed back to the organization in such a way that changes are made in inputs, throughputs, and ultimately product outputs which will now presumably satisfy customers better (1–4).

Let us now take dysfunctional organizations as I have discussed them in Chapter Eight of this book and conceive of them as open systems. In organizations, we often look for technical solutions to what are basically human or managerial dilemmas. When managers apply abstract, technical models like open systems theory to understand or rationalize organizing and production processes, no matter the product involved, there is always the danger that the mysteries of the human element will be underestimated. On one level, we always manage people by restricting their expression of subjectivity and their freedom. They have been hired to do a job, so they cannot do just whatever they want. They have to perform against certain goals. Yet the danger remains that if we remove human feeling and empathy from the work context, or if we ignore these elements and think of people as inputs or human resources, we distance ourselves from their humanity. In the long run, it can lead to the abandonment of our own.

To illustrate my point, I have changed the normal wording one might use to describe an organization that is functioning sub-optimally. I have done this to illustrate the device of *linguistic banality* that Hannah Arendt alludes to so effectively in her book on Adolf Eichmann (2003). Language is used to blunt the impact of dehumanizing elements in organizations. Applying our open systems model (Katz and Kahn 1998) to the organization and its members who fail to learn—a university, in this case—we have: (1) **The Inputs**—Faculty, students, books, tuition, pedagogy, technology, and facilities; (2) **The Throughput**—Students learning theoretical knowledge in conventional ways; (3) **The Output or Product**—Graduates capable of memorizing theory who are unable to take action on it or even to question the validity of their own theoretical assumptions; (5) **The Feedback Process**—Over a period of years, the process becomes more efficient and the feedback from the managers and organizations who hire these students is that they can neither think nor act to achieve results.

When No One is Home

When managers (or teachers) lack moral integrity, they have no inner benchmark that will tell them when they have stepped over an inner line into a mind space dominated by arrogance, self-deception, and a tendency to withhold their best selves from their employees (or students). This might or might not be a subtle thing. Think about how many human resources still work for companies that provide subsistence wages. In the United States, there is a free press, and journalists still use everyday language very effectively to convey the day-to-day horrors of man's inhumanity to man. One can read in the *New York Times* about a man or women being killed, or publically slandered, or fired unjustly, and we all know clearly what happened. If policemen beat black people with nightsticks, we see it on videotape. In the face of these facts, we appreciate that members of our society suffer. We sometimes become numb or immune to it because it is human nature to ignore what we might think we can do nothing about. Are we our brother's keeper? That of course is the sixty-four-million-dollar question. Where does our responsibility toward others stop and end?

Our answers to these questions might be determined by the language that we use. I will argue that the road to insensitivity begins and ends with language. Why is broad-scale job loss, which is still going on in 2016, often called downsizing, reengineering, or a necessary correction? Clearly, well-meaning people—executives, managers, professionals—use these terms. A single mom with three kids who has just been laid off doesn't talk about reengineering or downsizing. Laid-off, in fact, is a term that belongs in an earlier time when folks would be temporarily separated from the firm until work picked up again. There was an implied sense of obligation on the part of employer and employee to maintain the social compact. It was something of a cyclical phenomenon. It is curious that in an era of increasing misery for the have-nots—trending over the last twenty-five years—our terms for separating individuals from their organizations have become increasingly objectified, technologized, and sanitized. We might feel for these people, but how much do we really care? (I am asking myself the same question.)

Up to this point, we have addressed the first three questions: (1) What happens at the intersection of organizations and their geo-political context? (2) Are there forces in organizations that produce both performance and dehumanization? (3) How do you recognize the dehumanizing elements of organizations when you are experiencing them? We now turn to the final question: (4) What is the courageous and honorable way to behave when you feel trapped in a dehumanizing organization?

In the Belly of the Whale

Over the years, this writer has learned a few noteworthy things. One is to disbelieve the rhetoric of organizations. I suspect I am not the only one. George Herbert Walker Bush, our forty-first president of the United States, will always be known for his queries about the "vision thing".[10] A successful businessman himself, he didn't quite get it! I believe he didn't get it because of the inherent gap between the organizational ideals embodied in visionary leadership and traditional business values. The ideals of the humane visionary will often be seen, if ever, in a small segment of the strategic plan, in PR releases designed to persuade the public and customers of the essential goodness of the organization, or in vision statements which can be used for internal and external PR purposes. The vision statements are no real threat to the pragmatic/political realities of day-to-day operations, because they do not generate a tension in the consciousness of employees.

As an employee, I can believe in that vision statement without having to act on my belief. You can lay off people all around me, dump extra work on me to make up for the loss of slack, or cut my pay while top executives get bonuses. It seems that there is little I can do except complain or go elsewhere. I am unlikely to think of the idealistic principles of the organization's vision as a credo shared by all organizational members to which I can appeal for redress of grievances. I may even smirk indignantly at the gap between vision and reality. It helps, though, to remember that this is America, and I can always leave…right? Maybe, but remember, too, that this is a nation in the midst of global rightsizing. There are too few job openings out there, I am vested, and maybe the best I can do in these circumstances is to play it safe. In effect, I should be glad I have a job. I may, in fact, be powerless to effect any significant change. I want to protest, but everywhere I look, the door is shut. Management is not at home! Our leaders have left their better selves at the door. (I am under- or overstating the case, depending on your experience, for expository purposes.) In translation: My mind is incapable of taking in my current circumstances and responding with something other than victimhood or silence. I want to live my values, but I don't know how. Like Dilbert, cartoonist Scott Adam's insightful corporate employee (1997), all around me I see incompetence and wrong motives. Is there any action I can take, or have I created my own organizational prison, populated by manipulative guards (managers), constant isolation (personal withdrawal), and no exit (Sartre 1989)? I have boxed in and reduced my options to an unmanageable few, even though *I can leave at any time*. My personal perceptions and reactions to organizational life have taken control and I have compounded organizational abuse with self-abuse. What then can I do to break from this cycle of abuse?

The Exercise of Choice

As a beginning, I can carve out an area of psychological freedom for myself. I can refuse to see the organization as a monolithic presence that restricts my freedom. I can recognize that there are parts of the organization where I have control. If I am a manager with a job to do, I can stand back from that job or role and ask myself what I can do today, this minute, to act on my values…not just get back to work, but act on my values! Assuming you know what you value (care most about) in your life, you can bring at least one of those values into your life right now, this minute, and act on it. That will reduce the contradiction between

---

10 Mack, R. J. (2011). The Republican "Vision Thing". http://www.americanthinker.com/articles/2011/10/the_republican_vision_thing.html

the dictates of the organizational culture and what matters most to you. (I am not talking about surfing the Internet for hours; that is not a value but a pastime that steals from your employer; an addiction.) Let us assume you care most about your family and its wellbeing. At first glance, this seems to have little to do with work. On reflection, however, you can begin to see that your attitude toward work affects your relationship with your family. If you love them and want the best for them, you will want them to feel secure in the knowledge that you are an agent, not a victim, in your work environment. You will want to protect them from any abuse you are currently feeling, whether it is real or imagined. So you will stop complaining and whining about what you don't like and start to affirm that which is magnificent about your work.

Perhaps, like me, you are an academic and have time to write or reflect. Every day, I can choose to either focus on what I don't like about my university, and feel bad, or focus on the opportunity the university has given me to express myself in this rewarding way, thus enhancing my career prospects, and providing even better for my family. If my colleagues seem oppressive to me, if it dampens my spirit, I can choose to be around them less, by closing the door of my office, or I can ask them to lunch to get to know them better. If I am dissatisfied with the level of influence I have in the larger organization, I can apply for an administrative position or chair a committee. In other words, I can either challenge or accept my negative perceptions. By challenging those perceptions, I loosen their grip and hold over my behavior. I can challenge my perceptions and prejudices by acknowledging, if only in myself, that "I could be wrong about this person…I may not be seeing them in the right light…I may not be privy to the right set of facts." Or, "I could be wrong about myself in this particular instance. Maybe my motives are not as pure as I think they are or maybe I am not as gifted or competent as I believe myself to be in a given circumstance or role."

Here, I am forcefully and purposefully suspending judgment; I am doing what managers don't always get paid to do: considering the forces and patterns in life that may keep them from making quick, yet erroneous decisions. I am turning on my accumulated wisdom and wounds about a given individual or circumstance and calling them into question. In effect, I am looking at myself from the outside-in and saying, "Haldeman, you are not what you are cracked-up to be. You are not as stuck in your attitudes and beliefs as you think you are, and you do not have infinite freedom to impose your will on either people or situations. Neither victim nor Visigoth, you are really only free to be your best self. Everything else is a prison.

You were not made for bondage, whether imposed from the outside or within. You are free to face reality as it is; not as you would like it to be. Bondage is an artifact of childhood. Inhumane organizations are real enough, but neither organization nor individuals can really hurt you or shake your essential integrity, unless you let them. Your values and beliefs will play an essential role in determining whether or not you will let them. Victor Frankl (2006), existential psychiatrist and discoverer of Logotherapy, was a prisoner in Auschwitz for an extended period during World War II. He saw many people live and die. Some put their own spirits to death because they had lost all hope. In his book, *Man's Search for Meaning* (2006), Frankl argues that even the inmates of Auschwitz had choices as to how they would experience their oppressive environment. Hence, his oft-quoted and enigmatic reference to Nietzsche's statement: "He who has a why can cope with any how" (104).

To the Promised Land

In the end, as we consider the effects of global, societal, and organizational forces on the souls of men, we would do well to reflect on simple truths which bring joy in the face of adversity. Peter, Paul, and Mary, America's popular folk trio of the 1960s, may have said it best in their plaintive rendition of an old spiritual, *Michael, Row the Boat Ashore.* In this song, the River Jordan represents a natural barrier between man and the Promised Land. That river flows down through our organizations and cleaves them in two...on the one side, the old organization, and the false gods of profits, power, or security; on the other, our spiritual homeland. Our goal must be to ford that river:

> River Jordan is chilly and cold (hallelujah)
> Chills the body, but not the soul (hallelujah).
>
> River is deep and the river is wide (hallelujah)
> Milk and honey on the other side (hallelujah)

DISCUSSION QUESTIONS FOR SELF-EXPLORATION

1. When has the official point of view in your organization masked a tendency to distance administrative reality from the needs of people?

2. Think of a time when you personally used language to criticize or subtly abuse others in your organization (the goal, of course, to establish yourself as one-up and superior)?

3. Describe that situation. What justifications were you able to come up with at the time? How do you see it now?

REFERENCES

Adams, C. (1997). *The dilbert principle*. (Reprint ed.). New York, NY: Harper-Business.

Appuzo, M. (2015, March 4). Ferguson police routinely violate rights of blacks, Justice Depart. finds. *The New York Times*. Retrieved from http://www.nytimes.com.

Apuzzo, M., & Eligon, J. (2015, March 5). Ferguson police tainted by bias, Justice Department says. Retrieved from http://www.nytimes.com

Arendt, H. (2003*). The portable Hannah Arendt*. New York, NY: Penguin Group (USA).

Burke, P. J. (1969). Scapegoating: An alternative to role differentiation. *32*, 159–168.

Collins, J. (2001). *Good to great*. New York, NY: Harper Business.

Collins, J., & Porras, J. I. (2004). *Built to last: Successful values of visionary companies*. (First ed.). New York, NY: 2004.

Cummings, T. G., & Worley, T. G. (2009). *Organization development & change*. Mason, OH: Southwestern Cengage Learning.

Finn, P., & Warrick, J. (2009 March 9). Detainees' harsh treatment foiled no plots. *Washington Post*. Retrieved from http://www.washingtonpost.com

Frankl, V. (2006). *Man's search for meaning*. Boston, MA: Beacon Press.

Golding, W. (2011). *The lord of the flies*. New York, NY: Perigee Press.

Haldeman, J. (1991) Self-managed work teams: Why the right design matters. *Bay Area Organizational Development Network Journal, 10*.

Hamel, G. (2002). *Leading the revolution: How to thrive in turbulent times by making innovation a way of life*. Cambridge, MA: Harvard Business Press.

Kahn, R. L., & Katz, D. (1978). *Social psychology of organizations*. (2nd ed.). New York, NY: Wiley.

LaFraniere, S., Cohen, S., & Oppel, R. A., Jr. (2015, December 2). How often do mass shootings occur? On average, every day. Records show. *New York Times*. Retrieved from www.nytimes.com.

Mintzberg, H. (2005). *Managers not MBA's: A hard look at the soft practice of managing and management development*. San Francisco, CA: Berrett-Koehler.

Mydans, S. (1992, April 30). The Police Verdict; Los Angelas Policeman Acquited in Taped Beating. *New York Times*. Retrieved from http://nytimes.com.

Nuttall, T. (2015, November). The migrant mess. *The Economist, The World in 2016*, p. 95.

Porzio, M. (2015, October 22). Is record M&A activity sustainable? *Forbes*. Retrieved from http://forbes.com.

Sartre, J. P. (1989). *No exit and three other plays*. New York, NY: Vintage Press.

Kim, Sung Ho. (2007, August 24). Max Weber. In Stanford University Encyclopedia of Philosophy. Retrieved from plato.stanford.edu/entries/weber/.

Taylor, S. E. (1989). *Positive Illusions*. New York, NY: Basic Books.

Thompson, L. (2008). *Making the meeting: A guide for managers*. (3d ed.). Upper Saddle River, NJ: Pearson Education Division.

Tran, M. (2009, January 22). Obama signs order to close Guantańamo Bay. *Guardian News and Media*. Retrieved from http://www.guardian.co.uk/world/2009/Jan/22/hillary-clinton-diplomatic- foreign-policy)

Weber, M. (1978). *Economy and society): An outline of interpretive sociology*. Berkeley and Los Angelas, CA: University of California Press.

Zimbardo, P. G. (2007). *The Lucifer effect*. New York, NY: Random House.

INTENTIONALITY

Power Source for Meaningful Change

What We See is What We Get

In this chapter, I will argue that there are many types of change. Most of us believe we want transformational change: the kind that will lead quantum leaps in performance. It is not so much that we want to be transformed. It is that we want to have an organizational engine that performs at high levels, continuously. If it takes personal transformation, so be it! The author will argue that transformation, at either the personal or organizational level, is a laudable but elusive goal. The lynchpin upon which the structure of organizational transformation rests is the executive's ability to move beyond willpower, drive, and ambition to personal intentionality (May 1969). Like any phenomenon, multiple factors can promote or delimit an organization's ability to transform. All of these pale when placed next to executive intentionality. Intentionality flows from personality. It is not the same as the intention to act in a certain way (221). It is the capacity to imagine, to envision, to creatively participate in the coming day's possibilities. If we can see beyond what lies right in front of us to continuously ponder the deeper issues at hand, we can develop the capacity to shape our day and our own mindsets and behaviors by living in a creative space where we are at play in strategy, design, and action—all at once. This is sometimes called living in the moment.

Intentionality can be defined in two stages: (1) The preliminary stage is to understand that our intentions are decisive with respect to how we perceive the world (222). For example, a CEO might walk into a conference room full of 1,000 employees, intent on laying off a third of them. With that intention in mind, he or she is likely to perceive HR representatives and pink slips. The individual employees may simply disappear. Another CEO may walk into the same room with the intention of delivering a speech that will lift employee spirits (in the face of an economic downturn). This CEO may see committed employees he or she will depend on to improve sales and productivity, people who are loyal and who care. Each CEO's perception is different because the meaning of the situation is different to them. (2) The other side of intentionality comes from what is supposedly out there in the real world. Just as we perceive selectively, based on our intentions, so the world of people and objects influences us and further shapes the current contents of our perceptions. In the first example, above, if the employees respond to the CEO's speech with derisive laughter, the original intention(s) may shift. The figure/ground relationship has changed. The CEO might be thrown back by this interruption of his current intentions into a deeper set of meanings that lie within himself. Perhaps his heart will be softened as he recalls the times when his parents sacrificed to make sure he would be able to get a college degree. Maybe she will recall a childhood friend whose father was always getting laid off amidst the vagaries of industry cycles. The executive, maybe for the first time in decades, allows herself to link the remembered pains of her friend's childhood with the present-day event she has just experienced. For just a moment, deep empathy for her employees breaks through. The habit of excusing oneself with, "This is business," is now seen as an easy way out of what has become a sharply defined moral and ethical dilemma. Due to the dynamic interplay between subject and object, the meaning of the situation has changed for the executive. Intentionality acts as a bridge that expands executive and managerial consciousness. By extension, that same bridge will expand our own consciousness.

What is Change?

It is fashionable to regard external demands as the drivers for change in our organizations. Implicit is the notion that people will not change unless they see an external need. For example, we will not merge with another company until our company has demonstrated that it is unable to recover from a failing position. We will not address our turnover problem until our turnover rate has reached twelve percent a year (some executives even consider high turnover rates as a normal cost of doing business). Change is construed as the organization's reaction to what is happening in its immediate task environment. The model is a thermostatic one: When environmental conditions reach a certain critical mass, internal changes kick in.

Meta-Cognition

In contrast to this, and a polar opposite on the continuum of personal responsibility and accountability, is Model II change. Chris Argyris, professor emeritus at Harvard University (1990) developed the approach and has written about it extensively. This is change that can be facilitated by a good OD consultant. It has the potential to change both consciousness and behavior. Briefly, Argyris argues that once executives are confronted with their defensive and duplicitous communications patterns, by reviewing transcripts of their real communications behaviors, they can be helped to see the gaps between intention and reality. Their consciously expressed espoused theory of communication—what they say they believe or intend in their communications to colleagues—can be shown to prompt and evoke an unintended set of communication behaviors and responses (p. 13). That is because their actual behavior, which all individuals have a vested interest in defending, is what was received by the other. The implication is that once smart managers have their eyes opened about the effects of their personal behavior on others they will change! They can learn new, more open behaviors at both verbal and non-verbal levels. This will narrow the gap between intention and action. They can learn to operate at higher levels of thought—called meta-cognition—and deeper levels of self-honesty and self-awareness.

Human Encounter

Leaders of change—whether executives, middle managers, or external change leaders—can be seen as acting within the framework of this chapter. Change leaders help the people they work with to become aware of personality levels which influence behavior at the level of conscious intention. They often do this by simply pointing out what they see. Whether internal or external, change leaders are paid to point out the discrepancy between intention and action in the members of their immediate work force, for key stakeholders, and most of all, for themselves. It is only when we feel the tension between what is ideal about ourselves—the self we prefer to be—and the self that is tangibly real to others, will we be able to change. Otherwise, our own internal dialogues and personality structures will tend to reinforce the untruths and half-truths we tell ourselves. This is true for consultants, executives, middle managers, and the average employee. By facing the personal gaps between our own actions and intentions, and learning to understand the blind spots and mistaken perceptions of ourselves and others, we can all join the human race! We can own-up to our own failures and anxieties and accept the mistakes of both ourselves and our colleagues without judging anyone! This is called getting real. If we can learn to give each other clear feedback about specific behaviors and their effect on us, we create the condition for more informed choice for everybody. If I let you know your anger at me seems misplaced and that I feel offended, you now have a new awareness and a choice for how you will deal with me in the future. This approach to change ostensibly has the ability to upend individual and organizational defenses, to help people see themselves and others more clearly. Both middle managers and executives will learn to speak openly about matters that previously acted as inhibitors to meaningful organizational change. As noted earlier, at the level of the individual, this is called personal learning; at the level of the total system collective, organizational learning. In fact, one premise behind the new focus on organizational strategy mentioned in Chapter Five of this book is that dynamic interaction between organization and environment leads to new set of conditions, which call forth new strategies and behaviors from executives managers, and other employees. The same thing applies to all industries and organizations. In Chapter Eight, we demonstrated how effective strategic change (strategy formulation and implementation) required organizational learning (Argyris 1967; Argyris and Schön 1996). Now we mention another complicating factor: Organizational learning does not occur without the deepening of intentionality in the individual, team, and organization.

Change is What We Think It Is

Take, for example, two models of organizational change: Organization-as-thermostat and organization-as-learner. Organization-as-thermostat [my term] means that organizations attempt to keep their level of functioning stable, neither too effective, nor too dysfunctional. Anything outside of this range will cause pain and disequilibrium in the system. Organization-as-learner sets the bar higher. This type of entity wants to evolve and grow. In a certain sense, these types represent extremes on a continuum: The mechanistic/bureaucratic organization and the organic, adaptive organization (Burns and Stalker 1995). Both of these are meaningful metaphors for the ways in which organizations change or do not change. Over the past 25 years, both models have been very popular. These are but two of many alternative change models that exist today[1]. I present these two models or frames as a point of contrast to my own viewpoint, which rests on a different epistemology or way of knowing about change. My model has the advantage of stepping outside current frames and explanations to reconsider the experiential phenomenon of change. The question is: What is the meaning of change for individuals at any given point in time, and what actions will they either take or fail to take because of that meaning?

This is no idle question. There seem to be as many definitions for change as there are individual managers and executives. For example, I think that people and organizations—societies and the world, for that matter—are always changing. Change never stops! It is not something new and radical, an artifact of our Knowledge Age. It is perpetual and perennial

---

1   See Cawsey and Deszca, 2012, for a summary.

like the dawn. In organizations, we become active or passive over time or active and passive at the same time. We adapt or fail to adapt to new ways of doing things. Later, our level of adaptation may shift. We get confused as we attempt to sort out what is genuinely new or unique from what is merely novel. We recover. We think we are competent in a given skill set only to discover we are only partially competent. We can expect to become fully competent three months or two years from now. We accept reality; we deny reality. Through all this change continues. You are not the same person today that you were yesterday. The universe, physicists tell us, is perpetually in flux. So are you and I and our organizations. All this was going on well before global competition ever started. It will continue well beyond the point where global competition evolves into some new socioeconomic hybrid.

We lose our centers when we focus only on adapting to constant change or even on adapting to the acceleration of change. External change is not the only kind of change that matters. You and I are growing older every day; that is change. It's not sexy, but it is change. Somehow, in our culture and time, we are led to believe we must adapt to change, design for change, and, well, change, as if we really could do anything else. Is this a mantra that we must keep repeating until we reach a new level of manic awareness? Are we likely to change any more easily because writers of business books, management consultants, and psychotherapists tell us we must? In the midst of all this frenetic posturing, we might pause and ask, What kind of change do we mean? How relevant is it to who we are and what we do? What if the constant change mantra we all seem so obsessed with in our organizations is simply a lot of noise? What if we are missing the point because we don't know what change really is, and we wouldn't know it if we saw it? What if change is really all kinds of things going on at once that we don't fully understand and that do not lend themselves to simple conceptualization? To extend the point, we might even ask if the core concept, change, has implications for sub-concepts like no change, partial change, and changeless. Are we managers, researchers, and consultants accepting common, zeitgeist-derived understandings of change and its derivatives where no real understanding exists within our personal spheres of meaning and influence? Is it possible that at the level of personal experience, we still do not have much of a clue?

Elements of Change Theory and Practice

How is change different from development, or change management from organizational development? Or organizational leadership from change leadership? One is tempted to argue, "Whatever sells. Right?" Academic, theoretical distinctions do exist. Cummings and Worley, (2009) well-known researchers and consultants among others, have catalogued specific definitions and a variety of distinctions among terms. Again we ask, Do these have much meaning for the management practitioner or the executive mind? I must admit that as an administrator, teacher, and consultant, I have often found many change-related terms somewhat irrelevant to what I do. This is partially because, in the business world we often adopt popular definitions of change as a form of linguistic shorthand. Then, too, we use them interchangeably.

Change might mean that over time, nothing remains the same. This is the type of change I allude to on the first two pages of this chapter.

When we substitute one thing for another, that is also change. This is what some organizations attempt to parlay as transformation (the real thing). Substitution means we change a few props (maybe the language in a shared vision), we arrange the organizational stage to create a new setting ("all managers through 360° feedback by year's end!"). We are trying to get the audience to join us in a shared fantasy that will take us all out of present time and convince us that this is the way the world is (for a while). We want our managers to become bold and progressive (in the style of our least progressive executives)! No one cares to admit that the same old emperor is simply wearing a new set of clothes! Let's be frank: We are being entertained, and the play is, indeed, the thing! Managers use impression management and prop manipulation because it is much easier than leading their people through transformative change. In practice, it works something like Lincoln's, "You can fool all of the people some of the time." Used too often, this type of change in appearances will evolve into Lincoln's final rejoinder, "you can't fool all of the people, all of the time."

Cyclic change is another type of change. Consider industry cycles. These are recurrent, predictable changes that occur within an industry. They cannot be directly controlled but can be reasonably well understood. Through knowledge and planning, a form of control will emerge. One such cycle is increased consumer spending over the holidays. Retail stores can normally depend on this cyclical change, but in the wake of the Great Recession, it does not seem to be immutable. There are reduced industry cycle times today. Technical innovations in computer chip size, complexity, and cost have dramatically reduced the cycle times for production of new products across many industries. Such changes in industry cycles create more urgency for information gathering, knowledge creation, and planning. In principle, however, strategic planning and product and process innovations can manage the reductions in cycle times.

Transformational change refers to the type of change we have been experiencing since the early 1990s. This type radically upends and pushes us to continuously reframe our cognitions and perceptions (what we think and what we see). Reality morphs to intrude upon relatively fixed meanings and models in our minds.

Change and Management Control

The point is that all these kinds of changes are occurring simultaneously, yet only some of them are susceptible to management control as we have known it during the industrial era. Transformative change, global change, has accelerated over the last 40–50 years. Organizations and individuals, like animals in the sea, have been left to adapt or die. Managers have often been able to act in the face of these turbulent changes, but the industrial age metaphors of man dominating nature or other men have run their course. We are no longer able to beat our enemies into submission like we did in World War II or dominate the world's steel markets through new forms of protective tariffs. Afghanistan and the Gulf Oil Spill have become our new metaphors for dealing with the resistance of peoples to change and the powerlessness of managers to manipulate forces or determine direction. We have seen that while man and his organizations can be heroic, they are just as often tragic. The world is apparently our playground now, and like out-of-control toddlers, we are wrecking the playgrounds upon which we have built our sand castles.

Many private sector businesses have already made significant adaptations to change of the alteration variety. They change, they change, but they do not really develop or transform. Just as some adults never really develop beyond their teen years, so organizations may hold onto past values, habits, and practices. They have downsized. They have divested themselves of businesses they did not know how to manage. They have begun to learn how to manage teams. They have merged. Yet, fundamentally, the leopard never seems to have changed its spots.

As we have been discussing, meaningful change is different from simply adapting to external demands. It involves a substantial amount of looking inward. It is asking ourselves who we are; what can we be? What significant contributions do we want to make to the world and to our local communities? We need to do this individually and collectively. What do we have to offer? What are our competencies? What are our down-to-earth dreams that have a good chance of being realized, if only we will commit the time and resources to make them happen. From a more right-brain angle, "What would the lion in us want...the steed...the gazelle? Are we ready to let go of the ostrich, the bear, or the octopus in order to make it happen?

The answers to such questions are usually not readily apparent. This form of enquiry requires the generation of new, tacit knowledge that we carry around in our hearts as well as our heads! We have to move behind and beyond our customary individual and organizational defenses (Argyris 1990).

Human Dilemmas of Change

Organizations are man-made. They are a tool which man invented and uses to accomplish multiple purposes (Thompson 2003). The production of products and services is only the most obvious. Other purposes are to satisfy employee needs for meaning and compensation and to reinforce the wider cultural values of the societies within which they are embedded. In this latter sense, organizations are as much agents of the status quo as they are agents for change. As any executive can tell you, these various purposes often do not align with one another. This lack of alignment produces a certain noise or dissonance in the organization as a system.

Now add to this another lack of alignment: If man has a certain darkness within himself—an irrational self with its own needs, partially at odds with the rational persona presented at work—it will also make sense that man's organizations have hidden dimensions and strata of darkness. At the executive level, positive performance and stewardship-related values will conflict with executive narcissism and the will to power; at the cross-unit level, deep and abiding conflicts might easily proliferate; in teams and work groups, skewed group dynamics and dysfunctional norms will threaten group identity and high performance norms; at the individual level, distorted perceptions of self and others will drive out reasoned communication.

The Will to Self-Deception

Other examples of organizational darkness abound. Running throughout the organization, and shaped by its warp and woof, are half-truths and partial versions of reality. As man, we are creators and shapers of meaning. We purvey our meanings in language: written, spoken, and non-verbal. As executives we are not necessarily compensated for the truthfulness of what we say. Executive rhetoric, public relations framing, and lobbying efforts may be colored with lies and deception. This does not necessarily imply purposeful efforts to misrepresent the truth, although that may happen. It does imply, as Freud (1938) established, that part of the human condition is to misrepresent the truth about reality or to distort reality to preserve one's sense of self-esteem. We all lie to ourselves in the service of the self. "The truth at all costs!" is not the credo we live by. Rather, our credo is something like, "The truth when it is convenient, when we allow ourselves to see it, when it does not threaten our self-image or demand that we make ourselves vulnerable." If we stakeholders want to make meaningful change, we will have to entertain the likelihood that these types of organizational darkness will stand in our way. We will have to face them and take a stand against them.

Multiple Versions of Reality

Even if we do not intend lies and deception, we have to recognize that the numerous value perspectives and personal agendas, which exist in any given organization, will cause stakeholders to view reality differently and to see the objectives of meaningful change differently. There will be conflicts over personal meanings, identities, and definitions of reality. If we want to get at the truth about meaningful change and how to make it happen, we will have to confront this paradox: Whose version of the truth are we talking about, for what end, in whose service? If we want to transform, not just alternate or exchange one bill of goods for another, we must identity the sources of leadership, light, and vision that will guide the journey. We must also identify the elements of organizational darkness that are arrayed against us, and we must not underestimate the power and tenacity of existing levels of consciousness to undermine our best efforts.

Conflicting Models of Morality

Here is the vexing truth about our organizations and ourselves: We are all at war with ourselves and with our organizational fellows. We have a vested interest in not knowing the truth about our motives and values. We want to project our best selves to our colleagues, partners, and customers, but our dark underbellies betray us again and again. Hundreds of times, on any given day, in organizations around the world, managers face a common type of moral dilemma. The dilemma normally comes in the frame of an either/or decision. It is a decision over what to do in a mixed motive situation. One side of the decision is often principled; the other side is typically self-serving. Stated briefly, the dilemma is, "In this particular situation, where I have both something to lose and something to gain, what should I do? Should I do the right thing, meeting the situation head-on, seeing it through, come what may, or should I not rock the boat, protect my flank, manipulate my way out of this one, keep my distance because it may damage my relationships or career prospects?" An example of the type of problem is the difficulty executive change leaders face when they run up against a certain type of resistance to change (Cawsey and Deszca 2012). If they have worked with colleagues for long periods of time, as one often finds in academia, government, and health care, they often become curiously reluctant to confront saboteurs-who-have-been-friends…

even when those friends are working against their own best efforts. If a VP talks smilingly about the change project to their CEO but undercuts that same CEO in discussions with peers or direct reports, one sometimes finds, rather curiously, that the CEO may even know about this phoniness, yet choose to ignore it. As a consultant, I have often seen this happen. It may be easily explained when you realize that part of that CEO is still aligned with the status quo but has convinced himself that his old friend meant no harm. The organizational darkness I have been discussing has kept him glued to his old affinity network. Put another way, organizational blood has proven to be thicker than the inviting trickle of organizational change. The CEO may have good intentions and be good at crafting rhetoric for shared visions, but not so good at living up to it when his larger self remains embedded in a matrix of commitments to the organization as it was. Typically, he provides his own way out, justifying his refusal to confront his friends on the grounds of pragmatism. As George H. W. Bush would say, "It wouldn't be prudent!"[2] To this consultant, prudent always sounds a little like fear and preservation of the status quo. Executives are almost always pretty bright and their personal defense constructions are often quite sophisticated. Add to that the reluctance of others to question these or to risk penetration of their own personal defenses by making themselves vulnerable, and you have a pretty potent preservative for organizational darkness!

Demonology in the Twenty-First Century

Managers shape themselves and their organizations by the way they respond to dilemmas like this. Psychologist, Rollo May (1969), a shrewd observer of human personality and behavior, writes about **the daimonic**, natural instincts, which can temporarily take over the whole person (121). Sex, love, rage, and power-lust are examples. These forces will bypass or pervert reason, pressing our rational faculties into the service of instinctual appetites. This same daemonic is also the source of creativity, inspiration, and vision. If not overly constrained by repressive forces (in the individual, the organization, or the state), the flow of creativity can be nurtured and channeled into artistic works or management/worker innovations[3].

Leading with Vitality!

Tying to the theme from Chapter Two of this book, the lesson for managers is that creativity and innovation cannot be willed or driven only but must first be nurtured or grown. Organizational conditions must be right. The organizational climate must be temperate and not characterized by extreme management styles—neither too driven nor too faceless. Healthy conflict must be surfaced and faced, people and groups encouraged to engage one another. Employees must feel like there is a readiness to embrace the new and unique. They must witness management letting go of control long enough to perceive and embrace the daimonic within themselves, the deeper sources of intentionality and power. They must believe executives have the will to source their demons and tame them! Executive vitality

---

2 Retrieved from HARE-DANA-BUSH-SAYS-WOULDNT-BE-PRUDENT.html%3fpg%3dall/RS=^ADAvU0 2nkwXlMfGGatzxlHVLAlwSl8-

3 Retrieved from https://www.sonoma.edu/users/d/daniels/maylect.html

must be released and the depth of the intentionality within them deepened. Yes, behavior will need to change, but more than that, there will need to be a change of heart, an extension of personal consciousness and a cracking of the role shells that restrict their ability to tap their deepest selves. If the executives as a class are controlled and emotionally inaccessible, talk about change becomes a mocking parody. To talk about organization transformation in this type of wounded context is futile.

Transformative change, if that is what we want as leaders (we say it is) cannot be wrought by leaders who have gotten to where they are solely by a combination of intellect, drive, political manipulation, and bottom-line performance. While we might agree that these characteristics are important—in previous times, and under normal circumstances—we live in a time that is its own frame of reference. Executives whose most creative personal demons have been driven underground in the service of power, control, and the institutionalized status quo are not in position to provide the transformative leadership we need. They simply do not have it in them. They cannot attend to and explore those elements of their world and organizations that they have not faced and explored within themselves. They can cling to current adaptations and repeat the past. At their best they can force change through the system under a given time table which is simply a proxy for no change at all. People like this have lost the ability and the will to imagine, wish, and desire (May 1969). They are often unwilling or unable to properly invest in human creativity and innovation because they, themselves, have developed into gamesmen and women (Buchanan and Badham 2008): highly competitive individuals with a narrow focus on personal success and an inability to sustain truly intimate relationships with friends and colleagues. They remain unable to transform their organizations because the necessary personal development has not occurred. In certain cases, they might have a modicum of success while impoverishing their organizations. Other things being equal, it is about the best they can do.

Transformational Leadership

In summary, let us agree that the most meaningful change is organizational and executive transformation. We have proposed that executive transformation must occur if organization transformation is to occur. (In practice, these are curvilinear correlates, interpenetrating one another like a DNA helix.)

The matrix for this transformation lies in the depths of the individual executive mind (the preconscious and subconscious mind, if you are a Freudian). At the organizational level, we might speak of the collective unconscious (exactly as Carl Jung, psychiatrist extraordinaire, has spoken about the depths of the individual psyche). The collective unconscious equals organization darkness, as we have addressed it here. Unless the intentional levels of the executive personality and organization are penetrated, we do not have a chance of transforming anything. Unless we can tap intentionality as the power source for meaningful change, we will continue to tread water. The pull of internal and external forces mock our best efforts to manage that which is paradoxically unmanageable at the average level of executive consciousness! Put another way: There are no short cuts to transformation.

DISCUSSION QUESTIONS FOR SELF-EXPLORATION

1. Which challenges of intentionality do you think will be most relevant to your success? Least relevant?

2. How do you plan to meet these challenges?

3. Can you think of any circumstances where you may not be right for this job? If so, how would you face and act upon this knowledge? If not, why not?

REFERENCES

Argyris, C. (1967). Today's problems with tomorrow's organizations. *Journal of Management Studies, 4*(1), 31–55.

Argyris, C. (1990). *Organizational defenses: facilitating organizational learning.* Upper Saddle River, NJ: Prentice Hall.

Argyris, C. & Schön, D. A. (1996). *Organizational learning II: Theory, method, and practice.* Reading, MA: Addison-Wesley.

Buchanan, D. A., & Badham, R. J. (2008). *Power, politics, and organizational change: Winning the turf game* (2nd ed.). Thousand Oaks, CA: Sage.

Burns, T., & Stalker, G. M., (1994). *The management of innovation.* New York, NY: Oxford University Press, USA.

Change. (n. d.). *In Merriam-Webster's Online Dictionary.* Retrieved January 26, 2016 From http://www.merriam-webster.com.

Cawsey, T. P., Deszca, G., & Ingols, C. (2012). *Organizational change: An action-oriented toolkit.* Thousand Oaks, CA: Sage.

Cummings, T. G., & Worley, C. G. (2009). *Organizational development and change.* Mason, OH: Southwestern Cengage Learning.

Dana Carvey. (June 1, 2012). In *Wickipedia the free encyclopedia.* Retrieved from http://en.wikipedia.org/wiki/Dana_Carvey

Freud, S. (1938). *Basic writings of Sigmund Freud.* (A. A. Brill, Trans. & Ed.). New York, NY: The Modern Library.

Intentions. (n. d.). *In Merriam-Webster's Online Dictionary.* Retrieved January 26, 2016 From http://www.merriam-webster.com.

May, R. (1969). *Love and will.* New York, NY: Norton.

Thompson, J. D. (2003). *Organizations in action: Social science bases of administrative theory.* Piscataway, NJ: Transaction Publishers.

CHAPTER

GENDER, ETHNICITY, RACE, AND CLASS

The Specter of Class

Class is not a friendly word in our land of opportunity. Class analysis was supposed to have died with Karl Marx, yet it haunts us still [the author's opinion]. Class can act as a prism to illuminate our understanding of ethnic, gender, and racial differences, as well as other differences that can have an effect on relative standing. Before 2008, in the United States, global competition was in the foreground, global poverty in the background. Most people thought of themselves as middle class (Greenblatt 2010). Since then, the American middle class is developing a new appreciation for joblessness and the boundaries of class distinction. The specter of class is beginning to haunt us. The gap between the haves and the have-nots in the United States is widening. The rich grow richer, the middle class treads water, and the high school educated individual with no updated skill set has dropped into the economic ozone. This impacts each and every workplace, if only in the sense that individuals and groups with less money are unable to afford many products or services. Even in organizations that seem securely middle class, the people employed and the people served as customers can no longer take their economic security for granted. How long this will last, no one knows. Though women and minorities still receive legal protections in the workplace, widespread anxiety and malaise reduce openness of thought. Both managers and employees are unlikely to revert to the prejudice and abuse of an earlier time; the law, social evolution, and enlightened management has seen to that. Yet the progress in drawing creatively on their differences could easily be stalemated.

Diversity as Smokescreen

What I am seeking to introduce in this chapter and the one following is an appreciation of paradox and irony in the field that is currently called diversity and inclusion. I am convinced that these elements will have much to do with our ability to appreciate and harness differences in the work place. Paradoxes are apparent contradictions which turn out to be true. Organizations are paradoxical. People are paradoxical. Here is an example: In teams characterized by diversity, conflict is at the heart of creativity and innovation. If the members of these teams can harness conflict to a higher purpose and productivity, they will win the race. If not, they will simply be an aggregation of differing individuals who may even work against mission, vision, and goals.

Irony is nuanced denial. We are not taking what people say or do at face value. To speak ironically about diversity and inclusion is to state that the rainbow coalition in organizations is a mythic interpretation of race and class. In American society and organizations, we have noble aspirations about a race-blind, class free city on a hill. Our reality is still too often punctuated by memories of Ferguson and Baltimore in flames. This is the heart of irony.

The Denial of Gender Differences

Using a different example, consider Freud's classic question, "What do women want?" After all these years of psychoanalysis, feminism, and females in the work place, I would contend that, in general, men still do not know. After Equal Employee Opportunity Commission and affirmative action legislation, *The Feminine Mystique* (Friedan 2001), and decades of fighting for political, legal, and workplace equality, it is still unclear what impact these cultural shifts have had on workplace performance and the ability to capitalize on differences that affect organizations. Gender differences are arguably considerable. For the most part, organizations do not exist for the purpose of helping men and women understand their differences and similarities (with the exception, perhaps, of marriage counseling clinics, publishers of novels, and film studios).

Psychology and the arts reveal to us something that business norms portray as irrelevant to business processes and outcomes.

Corporate Social Responsibility

Business organizations exist to serve customers, shareholders, and employees, in a very context-specific sense. Society and its human relations dilemmas often come in a distant fourth place. It is only in the last twenty-five years that corporate social responsibility has come to the fore in a broad and sustainable way (Goodpastor 2005). Some executives might say that diversity is to be managed. The paradox is that in the name of equal treatment, conflict avoidance, norms of efficiency, and uncertainty reduction, managers curiously ignore very real differences, which could optimize work performance. Society and the law pays attention to these protected class differences and at least makes an effort to create a level playing field. Paradoxically, in defining the playing field, it is society and the law which most constrain innovative diversity and inclusion practices.

Compliance and Commitment

Compliance and commitment are two different things, and it is compliance that most constrains innovation and the experimental practices that accompany it. Most managers do not see themselves as harnessing protected class differences to the engines of competitive advantage, quality, and productivity. Strategic visions that say otherwise are seen as just words until the visions are enacted real-time.

Executives worry about the threat of disruptive innovations and wonder how colleges and universities can provide business competencies and seasoned graduates who will help them to undercut threats to competitive advantage. The exploitation and management of differences is often ignored except in fields like higher education, health care, government, and the most progressive business sector corporations. Awareness has increased significantly, but not necessarily action.

EEOC and Affirmative Action are compliance-based. A manager must do what the law says to be in compliance. Professions like Human Resources Management (HRM) are usually charged with enabling and enforcing compliance within individual organizations. OD as a profession espouses and practices the values of diversity and inclusion. When they consult to organizations, organization development professionals are likely to help institutionalize diversity and inclusion. OD practitioners and senior vice-presidents of HRM can help to align diversity and inclusion initiatives with strategic vision and objectives. Change leaders in general at the middle management levels and above tend to be ideologically and practically committed to diversity and inclusion. Openness, authenticity, diversity, and inclusion are key words belonging to the same reality map. Macro initiatives requiring commitment can temper micro processes and legislative mandates requiring compliance can open up the organizational system to culture change. The sustainability of such initiatives will depend on participating executives.

It is the executives who must embody the necessary organizational tensions, at least at first. Fortunately, executives have begun to support these initiatives when they perceive that the variety of programs and interventions seriously impact the organization's competitive advantage. To foster their commitment, it becomes essential to measure and evaluate results (Goodpastor 2005).

Diverse Stakeholder Groups

In this author's opinion, business organizations exist to produce both products and services for customers and to meet the wants and needs of multiple stakeholder groups. In this day and age, on average, there are at least eight different stakeholder groups that have the capacity to impact a given organization's effectiveness (Weisbord and Janov 2010) In schools, for example, one might find students, parents, principals, department heads, district leaders, staff, teachers, and taxpayers. These all have a stake in the mission and outcomes of the school (112). Beyond the notion of supporting diversity and inclusion internally, we now have to find ways to strategically envision a common future and find common ground that will sustain resource sharing, leadership, and learning over time, among the multiple stakeholder groups. The concept of synergy amidst complexity becomes essential. There is also the politics of change to consider.

Diversity and the Bottom Line

Today, diversity and inclusion are strategically tied to survival. We can never return to the past. Would we want to? Again, and paradoxically, the answer might be yes and no. Today's fast-paced work environment tends to drive out attention to diversity and inclusion. Even though effective teamwork depends upon it, the extreme task orientation of the modern business organization and the focus on rapid, results-oriented learning tends to undermine the appreciation and deployment of diversity initiatives. This requires a climate of openness and trust, and a personal stake in each other as well as in the team performance goals. Accelerated competition tends to create the opposite conditions:

Good for Diversity	Good for the Bottom Line
Encourage personal disclosure	Stay focused on work
Call people on their prejudicial remarks or behavior	Ignore all but most blatant incidents
Acknowledge differences	Let the law and HR policy substitute for learning and experience
Appreciate unique contributions	Hire a homogeneous workforce (Type A of all races, creeds, and genders)
Validate feelings	Banish feelings that don't conform to corporate norms
Question assumptions, challenge stereotypes	Rapid closure in communication; use of linguistic shorthand

| Locus of control through internal standards and values | Groupthink (Let's do it!) |
| Hire tempered radicals (Meyerson 2003) | External locus of control, bonuses, and stock options |

Expanding the Space for Knowing and Doing

Our time is characterized by a merciless passion for work and competition. It is a bloodless war of sorts, although the downsized might disagree about the bloodlessness of it.

Speaking truthfully and sarcastically, time is of the essence. We all have deadlines. "I don't have too much time for the soft stuff," a manager might think. The problem with such thinking is the generation of false dichotomies. It is not hard vs. soft skills. These two terms are beside the point. It is not even time vs. money. It is knowing and doing. If we do not get to know each other and the broader system at greater depth, we will never act in concert to deliver results.

We must create complex theories of the future in order to act deliberately. That takes time: reading, discussion, reflection, and action. Otherwise, we recreate the world of the past in present time. Given this reality, how can we practice the human relations tenets in the left-hand column—creating holistic organizations and the effective employment of diversity—when the elements in the right-hand column push us to conform. If diversity and inclusion are to have a chance, we must escape the boxes of outdated thinking that trap us in conundrums of our own making.

In the next chapter, I will argue that both protected class and other kinds of differences must be optimized in order to facilitate organizational learning and to compete effectively in the marketplace of products, services, and ideas. I am optimistic this will happen. If not, it is still up to every one of us to do the job, one person at a time.

QUESTIONS FOR SELF-ASSESSMENT

1. What specific differences stand out in your workplace?

2. How does your workplace fall on the two dimensions of organizational compliance and commitment to diversity? Create a two-by-two model with compliance on the horizontal axis and commitment on the vertical. Use a scale of 1–10 on each axis (1=low, 10=high), and plot your organization's location in the relevant quadrant.

3. How well do you think class distinctions explain behavior in organizations? What is an example from your experience?

REFERENCES

Alan Greenblatt. (October 6, 2010). Living in the middle class, falling behind? Retrieved from http://www.npr.org/templates/story/story.php?storyId=130248415&ps=rs

Freud, S. (1938). *Basic writings of Sigmund Freud.* (A. A. Brill, Trans. & Ed.). New York, NY: The Modern Library.

Friedan, B. (2001). *The feminist mystique.* New York, NY: Norton.

Goodpastor, K. (2005). *Corporate social responsibility: The shape of a history, 1945–2004* (Working Paper No. 1). Retrieved from Center for Ethical Business Cultures, http://www.cebcglobal.org/wp-content/uploads/2015/02/CSR-The_Shape_of_a_History.pdf

Marx, K., & Engels, F. (2008). *The communist manifesto.* Seattle, WA: CreateSpace.

Meyerson, D. E. (2003). *Tempered radicals: How everyday leaders inspire change at work.* Cambridge, MA: Harvard Business School Press.

Winthrop, J. (1630). City on a Hill. In *Digital History: Using New Technologies to Enhance Teaching and Research.* (Spring, 2016 ed.) Retrieved from http://www.digitalhistory.uh.edu/era.cfm?eraID=2&smtID=3

DIFFERENCES THAT MAKE A DIFFERENCE

Innovation as an Alternative

Premise—Organizations are built to suppress differences in the name of management. control, and execution. ("Let's get it done!")

Counter Premise—Organizations are built to maximize the expression of differences in the name of diversity and maximizing creativity.

Second Order Premise—Differences in the workplace must be valued, and the expression of these differences must be legitimized, facilitated, and harnessed to the work itself, for both legal and business purposes.

Leigh Thompson (2011), a distinguished management professor and expert on teams and teamwork, has made some major points about the importance of differences to team creativity, productivity, and innovation:

» In teams, surfacing minority opinions are important because they help the team "rethink the thought process about ideas, plans, and projects within the team" (197).

» "Teams with heterogeneity [differences] generate more arguments, apply a greater number of strategies, detect more novel solutions, and are better at integrating multiple perspectives" (225).

» "Teams in which members are diverse with regard to background and perspective, outperform teams on tasks requiring creative problem-solving and innovation" (225).

Why is this important for management and organizations? Innovation is arguably the major challenge for the United States as a society and for its organizations. Adam Segal (2011), a Senior Fellow for Counterterrorism and National Security Studies at the Council on Foreign Relations, has argued that, "The United States does have a powerful alternative to debt-fueled consumption. The resolution of some of the country's biggest challenges lies in innovation." Innovation is not just creativity, although creativity often precedes innovation. To innovate is to create something new, to make something in a new way. Innovators are dissatisfied with the tried and true. Americans tend to be good at innovation. It doesn't occur ipso facto or by fiat. It requires careful handling of both managers and employees, the valuing of their differences, and the opportunity to express those differences creatively, and within groups. It is the expression of differences that kindles the divine spark of innovation. While the individual, working alone, may be better at generating new and creative ideas (Thompson 2011), it is these same individuals working in groups, teams, and cross-team interactions who must optimize their differences in order to finally produce innovative, uniform products and services that can compete globally.

The Magic of Co-Creation

The basic argument of this chapter is that individuals, by expressing their personal uniqueness and appreciating the uniqueness of others will generate conceptual fire, an alchemy of disparate ingredients leading to products and services of pure gold. The differences among individuals can be valuable for organizational growth. Hence, differences make a difference! New ideas, means, and methods will emerge from the laboratory of co-creation. So while research shows that individuals tend to be more creative than teams in generating new ideas and solutions (Thompson 2008), it is in teams and organizations where these new ideas must be further refined and fermented in the crucible of public discussion and debate. When people with different backgrounds and experiences appreciate one another's humanity and perspective, the seeds of innovation are sewn, and what's more, these same people learn to subject these ideas to the discipline of organization and team goals, methods, and processes. By accepting, respecting, and valuing differences within the organization, the work itself is transformed, and it becomes easier to think of customers or clients as individuals with their own unique contributions in the co-creation of value (Prahalad 2004).

Innovation Management

To go beyond talent management and staffing as tired old solutions to brand new challenges, we need to do several things:

1. Create new products and services for new and existing global markets (easy to say; strategically complex)!

2. Develop recruitment and staffing practices that will attract prospective new hires who will bring diversity of background, thought, and perspective (not a slam-dunk but doable with existing knowledge, skills, and managerial courage)!

3. Innovate management practices that will provoke the expression of differences and the development of team and organizational norms that will protect people who risk contributing unpopular ideas or positions (an executive leadership role)!

Teams, Crackpots, and Innovation

Think of organizations as structures and networks of interlocking teams[1]. For the moment, throw aside the organization chart. Consider that in both functional and cross-functional teams, strategic and operational innovations are created. Innovation begins with ideas and creativity. The research shows that not just any old team composition will do this, or do it well. Homogeneous teams, teams of like-minded people, will often fail this test (Thompson 2011, 87).

Differences in EEOC categories are important, but also any differences in perspectives that will encourage doubt in what is and develop certainty that, with teamwork, it can be improved! Existing diversity in the organization's population and diversity that is introduced by recruitment and staffing practices make it more likely you will have individuals on the team "who will ask questions so fundamental that they challenge the premises of [what you've been working on] for the last 30 years" (Thompson 2008: 248). This is more likely to happen during times of fundamental change when disruptive innovations and industry shakeouts are stimulating both individual and group minds.

Recruiting and staffing for specific jobs and competencies is one thing. The first staffing filter you pass people through is their qualifications to do the work. There are also legal reasons to hire people in protected categories. This is not enough. If we want to include

---

1 Suresh Srivastva, personal communication, 1979

underrepresented groups—groups that have not previously been given sufficient voice in the organizational dialogue—we have to identify other differences that make a difference.

Naysayers Prompt Innovation

My position: It is essential to recruit and hire individuals who do not fully fit your particular organizational mold, individuals who are willing to speak-out and give voice to different perceptions of reality and different worldviews. These are people with strong identities who are not willing to deny their uniqueness in order to cooperate or get with the program; individuals who are willing to call into question prevailing norms, values, and behaviors. They will have strong boundaries and will resist intimidation that might come from embedded friends of the current culture.[2]

When we hire people, we talk a lot about, "Is there a good fit here?" Counter-question: "Do we mean the fit with the way things currently are (the existing culture and climate), or the way we want things to be, our emerging vision?" We need diverse people who have the ability to live in the organization as it is, while shaping the future. There is nothing wrong with tradition and values as aspects of the organization's identity. These act as anchors as the organizational ship wends toward its destiny. Yet I do not think we want our organizations to be too overloaded with or influenced by **traditionalists**. These people are often on the far right of organizational politics, and they tend to represent the 3 P's: prone to preserve their prerogatives. Most often we find that the people who have been here or in power the longest, are the ones most likely to value the organization the way it has been (there are exceptions; I speak in general). They might bring to the table the most valuable learning's from the past. They could be helpful in sustaining what is best about the organization. They are usually at least some of these people in key positions of power and influence. This happens because organizations are prone to embrace their identities—past, present, and future—warts and all!

Where we most need divergence and alternate points of view is in the search for the product, service, and social innovations that will ensure future survival and prosperity for all stakeholder groups. Traditionalists—in some organizations, the dominant coalition—might be prompted to innovate, but it is not prudent to hold one's breath. After all, they have made it this far by encouraging and adapting to what was. They are more likely to innovate and to take the calculated risks that accompany innovation when they are dynamically engaging with change catalysts (natural innovators) and other points of view. This creates a positive dynamic, which helps organizations change, and not just change, but face the future without rose-colored glasses.

Technology, change, and global collaboration are the central business topics that seem to be on everyone's mind these days; look at magazines, business books, and scholarly journals. We have to change because customer expectations are changing, the global economy and worldviews surrounding our place in the emergent world order are changing. Leadership

---

2 Be careful as you consider candidates. It is sometimes narcissists with little regard for others who are not afraid to speak out. The litmus test? Narcissists see the world as a reflection of themselves. They rarely listen carefully to what others have to say.

and change is the big challenge for us all. Without optimizing differences that make a difference, without supplementing the guardians of our organizations with social and product innovators, we risk remaining embedded in the past—calcified—an organization unwilling to change its fundamental assumptions about self and world. If I may say it quietly, this is one definition of insanity.

Trusting that I have at least made a case that diversity and innovation are linked, I will presently provide a few examples of staffing for this key strategic advantage. First, though, a summary charge to organizations—a warning: Grow up, mature, develop, learn, and throw away bad habits of mind and behavior that no longer work! Get moving! It's later than you think. Examine your past experiences and point of view, take what is best, **leave the rest**.

How Tempered Radicals Push the Limits

Debra F. Meyerson, Consulting Professor of Organizational Behavior at Stanford University, has written about Peter Grant, an African-American recruiter at a large bank in the Midwest[3]. Over 30 years in his job, he made it a personal and professional goal to hire people of color. Before he did, he had conversations with them, sharing his goals and dreams about changing the organizational culture. He expected them to agree to broaden the parameters of inclusion when they were in a position to hire. Using this approach he was able to hire 30,000 people of color over 30 years. Think of it, he did not directly challenge any crucial norms or policies in the organization by recruiting people who shared his values and beliefs. He was a quiet, patient revolutionary. He did not ask permission. He did push the envelope on what it meant to staff an organization.

Meyerson called these people tempered radicals. They are corporate and organizational professionals who work toward positive change in both their work environment and in the way their company conducts business. Often they accomplish their goals in ways that are just short of getting them fired. They are often, but not always, quiet leaders who act as catalysts for new ideas, alternative perspectives, organizational learning and change. They balance allegiance to core values and individual rebellion.

We read so much about the need for change in organizational cultures because current culture is often the greatest impediment to the execution of new vision and strategy. There are two primary ways to seed culture for diversity and creative exchange of ideas: (1) Staffing practices that promote diversity and (2) leadership practices that facilitate the expression and orchestration of diversity and inclusion. Either, by itself, will not do the job.

Staff and Lead for Diversity

Staffing according to traditional diversity categories of race, gender, and age, will introduce visible diversity into the system. For purposes of organizational change, that will not be enough. It is true, if we have been lopsidedly recruiting white males into good-old-boy networks, we will certainly want to hire more Asians, Hispanics, Afro-Americans, and international candidates

---

3 2001, Oct 10. Tempered radicals: How people use difference to inspire change at work. *Harvard Business School.* Retrieved from http://hbswk.hbs.edu/archive/2538.html

who will be promoted into responsible positions of influence. We will want more qualified women. In such cases, it is important to expand our criteria of inclusion for both legal and business reasons and to redress past grievances. If beyond that, we want a change-ready organization, we will need to do three things: (1) Select people with inquiring minds who will have a certain loyalty to the organization but will speak their minds, (2) identify current employees who are willing to express counter cultural opinions for the good of the organization, and (3) incorporate new organizational norms and practices that will make it a safe, inviting place for these people to express themselves, verbally, or in action. We must learn to expect it!

Mix Divergent and Convergent Learners

How do managers and human resource professionals identity the appropriate selection criteria or know these people when they see them? This is not a science, but we have some clues: Look for diversity of background as well as a list of competencies required for the job and integrate the two things loosely in your mind. At the risk of over-simplifying, my experience has been that organizations tend to reward more convergent thinking and behaviors that lead more directly to desirable outcomes (insight gained from consulting and administrative experiences in over fifty organizations). Many managers have been trained in more traditional business disciplines, such as accounting, finance, operations, or engineering. Marketing and HR managers may not fit this profile, but their corporate experience and bottom-line responsibilities will also tend to push them in the direction of convergence in thought and decision making. The role demands seem to reinforce convergence (thinking in tightly defined categories) over divergence (thinking in loosely bounded categories) (Kolb 1983). Convergence emphasizes decision, action, and implementation, drawing linear conceptual and action boundaries around a situation. Divergence emphasizes the ability to apply ideas from one categorical domain, such as outer space, to a categorical domain within the organization, such as virtual communication (Synectics 2016). The metaphorical connections between the two domains promise creative applications, although at times it may be necessary to force-fit those applications. The very practice of the creative discipline—which can be taught— will force the executive out of the box! The box will no longer seem so congenial. We are only beginning to learn that the strategic demands of the executive role and the necessity of adapting to continuous change require real-time management training and development in divergent or lateral thinking processes.

Wild and Crazy as the New Norm

Returning to our discussion thread, all of this is to say that these relevant but unusual staffing recommendations may not come naturally to the executive/managerial mind. They may well seem wild and crazy. Nonetheless, thinking this way has the advantage of reframing the context for the respect and utilization of differences. Here goes then:

1. Hire seasoned ministers of the gospel who want to work for your organization as a second career—step outside of conventional categories in your thinking. Many preachers are accustomed to saying what is on their mind from the pulpit, even if it ruffles feathers!

2. Look for evidence of the capacity for reflection as well as for action (a former small business owner with a degree in philosophy and psychology who has also served on boards of directors). These are sometimes called reflective entrepreneurs (Buchanan and Badham 2008).

3. "Evidence mounts that it is our soft sides—not our macho characteristics—that significantly contribute to career performance" (Steenbarger 2015, retrieved from http://www.forbes.com/sites/brettsteenbarger/2015/05/24/women-in-finance-the- soft-side-as-a-hard-asset/#ad8f4326915e, paragraph 7).

4. Guidelines seem clear: When you are interviewing two or more equally qualified candidates for a job, hire the person with the soft skills. It is a no brainer.

5. Consider hiring Ph.D.'s in Organizational Sociology and Systems Thinking for management jobs (a strong research and consulting background can help to incorporate this type of innovative perspective in management and the workforce).

6. Create interview scenarios or ask questions designed to test for atypical, unique or innovative responses to management dilemmas: "If the President of the company invited you into their office and asked you for advice on how to change this company, what would you say?" Individuals with unique perspectives are often able to recommend action strategies that step out of the "role box" they are being slotted for. Their responses may seem bold or politically incorrect, but what are you hiring for, the ability and courage to innovate or the ability to read the organizational tea leaves?

Over time, you will come to recognize these people. They are well qualified for the job but their primary contribution might be that they come from diverse, unconventional backgrounds. You may not be quite sure that they will fit. Actually, that is a good sign you ought to consider hiring them. Those employees whose primary motivation is security will never leave you with that impression.

Create Cultures of Innovation

In some cases, they will be members of protected classes with observable differences, but it may be their cultural, background, and cognitive/perceptual frames that make the biggest difference to organization practices and endgame. Their value lies in the very fact that they cannot and hopefully do not wish to make a work home in the organization as it is. In certain positive (not destructive) ways, they are at odds with the organization as it is! They are much more likely to help lead positive efforts to turn your organization into the best it could be.

Aside from considering tempered radicalism, there are some other populations you might want to tap for diversity. Richard Florida (2003), Head of the Rotman Prosperity Institute at the University of Toronto, argues that there is a Creative Class whose members bring high-level creative talent to the workplace. He has defined and researched the characteristics of the two major sub-classes:

1. The Super-Creative Core, comprising 12% of the workforce. It includes a wide range of occupations, including scientists, engineers, programmers, educators,

researchers, art designers, and media workers. These people "fully engage in the creative process" (69). They are innovative, creating commercial products and consumer goods. In their work, their primary function is to be creative and innovative, problem (and solution) finders.

2. The Creative Professionals, 18% of the U.S. workforce. These are the classic knowledge-based workers, those working in health care, the legal sector, and education. They draw on complex bodies of knowledge to solve specific problems, using higher degrees of education to do so.

The implication of this research for diversity is that a sample of these people should be recruited in every organization in order to promote a culture of innovation. (A caveat is that they are not likely to stay in organizations that do not value their contributions.)

Ray and Anderson (2001), a sociologist and a psychologist, have argued that 50 million people in the United States (one quarter of the adult population at that time) belong to a group called Cultural Creatives. There are two types:

1. Core Cultural Creatives – 25 million people, 12.5% of the adult population These are the more educated leading-edge thinkers. They are most often artists, musicians, psychologists/psychotherapists, alternate health care providers, and other professionals.

2. Green Cultural Creatives – 25 million people, 12.5% of the adult population The secular and extroverted wing of the Cultural Creatives. They follow the opinions of the core group and tend to have a more conventional religious outlook.

Here are a few characteristics and values of the Cultural Creatives that may contribute to the desirable diversity of your organization:

» They care about relationships and developing the gifts of others (desirable for teamwork and synergy).

» They have a global point of view and appreciation for other cultures and ways of life (directly applicable to tolerance and willingness to value differences in the workplace).

» They show deep devotion to personal development (applicable to willingness to change behaviors in the workplace, to learn, and to collaborate— drives out blaming behavior).

» They are optimistic about the future, want to be involved in creating new and better ways of life.

» They are concerned about the way big business sometimes generates profits, including massive downsizings, destroying the environment, and exploiting poorer countries (shows a concern for people, the environment, and global issues that could positively impact the workplace. In 2011, this became a leading-edge issue.)

» They like people, places, or things that are different (sometimes called cosmopolitanism; a concept related to diversity).

» They are concerned with authenticity: having their actions reflect their values, words, and beliefs (authenticity itself is one of their core values; values are the best predictors of actual behavior in the work place).

- » **They are engaged system thinkers and action learners. They act on their values and experiment with changes in work and work arrangements** (what more could a savvy executive want?).
- » They balance vision and action.
- » They are concerned about giving to, not just taking from, the organization.
- » **They are not easily pegged**; neither progressive nor traditional (this, alone, probably indicates that they are continually developing and learning).
- » **They represent a new synthesis; they are invested in a new and bigger global whole.**

As with tempered radicals, who these people are may even matter more than what they do. They are alternative models for what it means to be a contributing organizational citizen. These issues are germane to staffing for diversity because, while it illegal to discriminate in hiring on the basis of race, gender, ethnicity, age, or religion, it is not illegal to discriminate because a job candidate does not fit a particular organizational culture profile. We are free to screen out divergent thinkers or socialized deviants. The message of this research is that we do so to our competitive disadvantage and at our peril. We stifle both expressions of difference and dissent and also power enthusiasms and initiatives.

In summary, my message is that uniform products and services are good for customers, but what they desire from the organization will change over time. The organization will need to engage in ongoing transformation to respond to these changing desires and to cultivate new niches in the marketplace. This will require that the very best thinking and diversity of perspectives be brought to bear to ensure ongoing creativity and innovation. Message to Management: Do you want a culture of innovation? Then seed your organizations with innovators and create structures, systems, processes, and management practices that will channel and facilitate the creative clashes of multiple perspectives. Don't anchor your business in the thinkers of the past, but create forums for real-time discussion and deliberations where all viewpoints are welcome and where the only sin is the refusal to openly engage! I know; it's not practical or realistic, but the future of your organization may depend upon it.

DISCUSSION QUESTIONS FOR YOU

1. Individuals: If you find yourself having different values, and beliefs, a different Story from the majority in your organization; if your point of view is counter cultural and unique; will you be pressured to conform and downplay your personal truth, or will you challenge the status quo?

2. Managers and Teams: Are you willing to recruit and staff with qualified individuals who are not only different in race, gender, age, and religion but who present themselves as confident to question the status quo, not just rhetorically, but by taking risks in support of their differences? Give examples.

3. If you are not doing this, what is holding you back? How can you get past any tentativeness you may have?

REFERENCES

Brown, D. R. (2011). *Experiential approach to organizational development* (8th ed.). Upper Saddle River, NJ: Prentice Hall.

Buchanan, D. A., & Badham, R. J. (2008). *Power, politics, and organizational change: Winning the turf game* (2nd ed.). Thousand Oaks, CA: Sage.

Forida, R. (2003). *The rise of the creative class.* New York, NY: Basic Books.

Kolb, D. A. (1983). *Experiential learning: Experience as the source of learning and development.* Englewood Cliffs, NJ: Prentice-Hall.

Meyerson, D. (2001). Tempered radicals: How people use difference to inspire change at work. *Harvard Business School: Working Knowedge for Business Leaders Archives.* Retrieved from http://hbswk.hbs.edu/archive/2538.html.

Prahalad, C. K., & Ramaswamy, V. (2004). *The future of competition: Co-creating unique value with customers.* Boston, MA: Harvard University Press.

Ray, P. H., & Anderson, S. R. (2001). *The cultural creative: How 50 million people are changing the world.* New York, NY: Three Rivers Press.

Segal, A. (2011). *How American innovation can overcome the Asian challenge.* New York, NY: Norton.

Synectics (2016). *Synectics:30 years creating workforce options.* Retrieved from http://www.synectics.com/index_2.php

Steenbarger, B. (2015, May 24). Women in finance: The soft side as a hard asset. *Forbes Magazine Online.* Retrieved from http://www.forbes.com/sites/brettsteenbarger/2015/05/24/women-in-finance-the- soft-side-as-a-hard-asset/#ad8f4326915e

Thompson, L. L. (2008). *Making the team: A guide for managers* (3d ed.). Upper Saddle River, NJ: Prentice Hall.

Thompson, L. L. (2011). *Making the team: A guide for managers* (4th ed.). Upper Saddle River, NJ: Prentice Hall.

In the United States, in 2016, many hold the federal government in ill repute. There are many reasons; some irrelevant to this discussion. One likely cause is this: In the last 15–20 years, the Knowledge Era, the era of information technology has been punctuated by the acute convulsions of a global system experiencing the equivalent of a heart attack. The political parties seem to have polarized between the ideologies of "government is essential to solving our problems" and "government itself is the problem". Our leaders at the highest level balance their time between attending to reelection, posturing for the camera, and their constituencies, genuinely solving problems, and pleading "not my fault" when problems do not get solved. Frequently all of these things are happening in both an integrated and fragmented way, at the same time. Another curious thing is happening as a subtext: We have begun to doubt whether any group of leaders can govern this situation!

The Schools of Labor Relations

Against this foundation of conflict and complexity at the top of our political system, John W. Budd (2008), a labor-relations professor at the University of Minnesota, has argued that there are now unique opportunities for managers and employees to invent a new balance in labor relations. To support his argument, he presents historical context and frameworks for viewing labor relations (35–68). There are four major viewpoints: (1) The Neo-Classical Economics School; (2) the Human Resources Management School; (3) the Industrial Relations

School; and (4) the Critical Industrial Relations School. I will review these frames for the pragmatic purpose of substantiating earlier claims I have made in the book that conflict and differences that are worth holding onto and that there is no significant change without them. I will make the point a final time; with gusto, I hope, that command and control and managerial ideology are bankrupt myths that will not seem to die. I am on a mission to support a viable alternative and send them on their way. First, a review of the schools to make the case for change:

The neoclassical school of thought views organizations, managers, owners, and individuals as rational actors, self-interested agents operating in competitive markets, with perfect information to compete (42). Nations compete, economic blocs like the European Common Market compete, organizations compete, and individuals compete. In this social construction, markets and financial outcomes are what matter.

The human resources management school used to be called personnel management. In this context, labor relations is optimized by enlightened managers who care about employees and will address their wants and needs through progressive management practices (45–47). One of these might be quarterly feedback on job performance.

Very pointedly, and over and against the managerial focus of the neoclassical and human resources schools, the industrial relations school argues that bargaining power between managers and employees is **not equal** (47). Unlike in the neoclassical school, competition is seen as imperfect and employers are seen as tending toward monopoly powers. In this model, workers are the losers. They face ongoing unemployment when business conditions change. This can only be changed by creating a power balance between employees and managers. Hence the proliferation of unions in the mid-twentieth century (48).

Not to be outdone, the critical industrial relations school argues that the people in power—those who support the dominant ideology of a society—can both design and control institutions and organizations, which serve their own interests (49). When economic conditions are favorable, a rising sea may lift all boats, but the critical school would argue that temporary income redistribution is an artifact of national and global prosperity. When conditions change—as in our current economic mega-transition—class differences will reemerge. This is simply another way of saying that the capitalist and managerial classes have shaped society and its institutions to their benefit (49). According to this school, the only possible redress is worker control. One can clearly see that the critical industrial frame, like the classical view, can easily become an ideological position. The human resource and industrial relations frames can become ideological but are more subject to reality testing from day-to-day experience in the organizational trenches. Put differently, the neoclassical and critical frames start out with theoretical, visionary premises and are more likely to hold on to them in the face of evidence that does not necessarily support the initial premises. The human resource and industrial relations frames are supported by a more loosely held set of premises and are more likely to reconsider them in the light of new evidence. For purposes of this discussion, it is also relevant to know that the industrial relations position and frame forms the basis of our current system of U.S. labor relations law. Implicit in our legal codes is the notion that management and labor have different interests, which should be balanced through a process of bargaining and negotiation (Budd 2008, 48). The current system of government in the United States, and in many other countries, does not question the right of unions to exist. On the contrary, it fully supports that right (58). Put bluntly, in the words of Professor Budd, "U.S. laws pertaining to labor unions and collective bargaining reflect the central belief of the industrial relations school that unions are needed to counter corporate bargaining power and provide industrial democracy" (58).

Industrial Relations Frame as Truth Filter

With this backdrop, I return to my initial example of growing disdain for government in the United States. This trend was played out at the federal level in the summer of 2011. In this chapter, I intend to show that, while all four frames have some validity, it is the industrial relations frame that often prevails in all sectors and industries, whether explicitly or implicitly. Whatever the espoused theory of management, it is no accident that we still have managers and employees in most organizations. The terms themselves connote a distinction in authority and a power distance that can easily subordinate the interests of employees. Legal protections for employees came out of the IR school and implicitly recognize the relative lack of power inherent in the role of the individual employee. When communications breakdown occurs between management and employees—yes, even in the most progressive organization—it is clear to perceptive outsiders that the interests of certain groups—often employees—are either being misinterpreted or ignored. When this occurs, both managers and employees get caught in a trap, often of their own making, which involves a scramble for power:

From the employee perspective, this might look like, "I need to show you that there is a plurality of interests, here. I am not management and management is not me. You cannot take me for granted. I will be respected and reckoned with. I don't believe you will do that out of the goodness of your heart. By the way, you have shown me that it would be stupid of me to trust you!"

From management we might hear, "They ought to be grateful they have a job. Why don't they stop grumbling and do that job? There are plenty of people out there who would be happy to be doing what they are. I have a couple of really good people working for me, but a few bad eggs are ruining the whole bunch."

If you look closely, you will see that people from both groups are implicitly beginning to bargain for their interests, although in a somewhat dysfunctional way that often does not lead to positive resolution.

In nonunion organizations, there will often be a system of due process, owned and delivered by management or their surrogates (yes, I mean the human resources department). HR will assist management in interpreting and complying with the legal protections and constraints, and they will help employees use the protections afforded by the system to resolve these differences, but in the absence of a union, I would argue that management is still in charge (am I wrong? contend with me, please). The effectiveness of the system will depend on management's philosophy, attitudes, and good will. Can they empathize with the interests of the people who work for them to the point where they will put their own interests aside to fully address issues of equity (fairness) and voice (the opportunity to express one's point of view, even if somewhat radical)? Will management even be able to guarantee organizational efficiency if employee interests are subordinated or neglected? Lack of a union could mean that employee interests are being addressed in an effective way. This is often the HR position. It could mean that people are too cowed to organize. This is the critical industrial relations frame. It could mean that both employees and managers have endless options outside the organization, which is operating under conditions of perfect competition, and demand for labor is high. (Don't worry. Be happy.) This is the neoclassical economics point of view. Oh, yes, and it could be that everyone is in a state of denial.

Power Differences Matter

I hope to provoke the reader here: In this chapter I will show how the IR frame plays out at the highest levels of government, that mixed motive situations like this occur in organizations and societies of all kinds—particularly under conditions of high stress and uncertainty—and that there could be a central role for institutionalized interest groups (we could call them **stakeholder groups** if we don't like the old word union, with all of its conceptual baggage). All interest groups, inside and outside organizations, have a stake in exploring the limits of common and differentiated interests at times like these. What does this mean? It means that real-time, and in the heat of battle over issues that matter to all parties, everyone has to look for new ways to step outside current philosophies, mindsets, and habits to push the limits of cooperation. Is this really so different from what is happening right now as the world faces a series of intractable problems, almost none of which can be solved taking a completely self-interested point of view? Is this really so different from what happened several years ago between the executive and legislative branches of our federal government, ostensibly over the question of raising the debt ceiling but arguably over the question of who is to govern? I don't think so. How will this work in practice? I do not know. That is what I intend to explore in this chapter.

The IR Frame in National Politics

We saw the IR frame operating during the last weeks of July, 2011, in Washington, D. C., with the budget limit standoff. It is apparent this was the frame, mostly because we have a political system of separation of powers where bargaining and negotiations occur all the time. Theoretically, as in the labor management context, each party has separate but equal powers. More than that, we saw both the limitations and a misuse of the IR model as conventionally employed in the past. The Tea Party, a powerful interest group on the Republican side, approached what would have normally been seen as an opportunity for bargaining and compromise (IR school) through the prism of neoclassical economic theory.

The question for consideration: Under what conditions do we agree to raise the debt ceiling of the United States of America so that it does not default on its fiscal obligations? Presumably, all stakeholder interest groups agreed that it would not be prudent to default. This is something all involved parties seemed to have in common that would be likely grounds for the use of bargaining and negotiation tactics. It meets the litmus test of a mixed motive situation as defined by Budd (2008) in his classic text: "A mixture of conflicts of interests and shared opportunities for mutual gain" (270). Georg Simmel (1971) the brilliant nineteenth-century sociologist has elaborated on the utility of this mixture in maintaining social cohesion and a unity of purpose. This is particularly true in situations where involved parties might otherwise withdraw (psychologically, if not physically, as the executive and legislative branches of government have done over the last few years) (75). Simmel comments on the glue-like nature of the conflict/unity matrix:

> Hostilities not only prevent boundaries within the group [organization] from gradually disappearing...beyond this they are of direct sociological fertility; often they provide classes and individuals with reciprocal [give and take] positions which they would not find or not find in the same way if the causes of hostility were not accompanied by the feeling and the expression of hostility...The disappearance of repulsive (and considered in isolation, destructive) energies does by no means result in a richer and fuller social life (as the disappearance of liabilities results in larger properties) but in as different and unrealizable a phenomenon as if the group were deprived of the forces of cooperation, affection, mutual aid, and harmony of interest.

Neoclassical Ideology and the Framing of Reality

Consider this possibility: To get elected in 2010, Tea Party candidates preached the rhetoric of neoclassical theory (Budd 2008, 42–44) to the supposedly forgotten masses of alienated

American workers, small business owners, individuals with rural zip codes, the religious right (Jerry Falwell's old moral majority), and any others who were willing to step outside the social compact as institutionalized in our current interpretation of government power and functions. They did this by calling people back to the U.S. Constitution and the intentions of the framers (not a bad strategy, but complicated by the apologetics of Tea Party spin-meisters). They appealed to the supra-values of American individualism, states' rights ideology, and the implicit heroism of taking a rebellious, radical position. Creating a common enemy for the electorate to rally around—the federal government—they promised to eliminate big government and its excesses once they got to Washington. Interestingly, they defined themselves as the real Americans, making common cause with our revolutionary forefathers.

If government is the enemy and all the rest of us are free agents able to contract our services at will and compete in the marketplace, this sounds idyllic. If market forces left untrammeled will produce good paying jobs just because perfect competition implies it, and if government regulation is anti-business in principle, not just in the particulars, then the Tea Party group is onto something. We would do well to take heed. Alternatively, we should consider that this rhetoric is just what the "Don't mess with Texas" value proposition implies, "Leave us alone, and we'll do it ourselves." The world has become extremely complex and interdependent. Conflicts, complications, and entanglements exist. We cannot go home again.

The Tea Party has simplified our national debate by taking an overly simplistic position. By leaning almost exclusively on a neoclassical set of assumptions, they have allowed this belief system to prevent them from compromising within a system that they are a part of, built on IR (mixed motive) premises, and depending for its workability on the willingness to bargain and negotiate.

Cultural Contradictions Add Complexity

To stay with our political example a bit longer, it is worth considering how the conflict/unity dynamic can evolve in situations where the interests in conflict have become polarized, as in the example above. Such situations seem fueled by the pursuit of causes. We have explored earlier in this book the complexity of global systems of economic, social, and organizational interdependence where there are many forces operating, all in dynamic interplay and evolving toward an uncertain outcome over time. The thought models seem to tax the limits of human ingenuity and adaptability. Harvard Sociologist Daniel Bell (1996) has added to this complexity by arguing that western capitalism in its current form is characterized by three contradictions: (1) The tension between work and consumption (283); (2) the tension between middle class behavior and politics and post-modern rejection of limits and norms (283–284); and (3) the tension between legality and morality (284). Because these themes will be linked to my discussion of industrial relations, I will address each in more depth:

(1) Work and Consumption – The Protestant work ethic originally reinforced hard work, the accumulation of capital, and reinvestment in the business (Weber 2008). Over time, the goods and services spawned by the growth of capitalism required an emphasis upon the consumer/acquisitive impulse so that these products could be sold. The more growth in the economy, the greater the requirement for persuading potential purchasers to buy. Over time,

the value of production was superseded by the emphasis on consumption. Our system in particular came to depend on it. National habits changed: Pleasure, debt accumulation, and refusal to defer gratification increased in public esteem. In the West, we are currently seeing the natural culmination of this cultural contradiction (283).

(2) The Middle Class and the Postmodern Revolt Against Standards—This theme means, rejecting the past, committing to ceaseless change, and holding nothing sacred and inviolate. The trending has continued right up to the present day. As I have noted earlier in this book, we have been bombarded by the word change from all forms of media and bully pulpits so that the term itself has ironically come to mean very little, or nothing at all! The 2016 iteration is that the middle class is shrinking and that profanity in literature and the cinema has become a form of high art. We have come a long way from Holden Caufield who at least had the excuse that he was going through an extreme form of adolescent rebellion and alienation. (Ironically, the author of *Catcher in the Rye*, J. D. Salinger, turned his back on notoriety retiring to the woods of New Hampshire to live a more contemplative life in an atmosphere of vivid natural beauty and continuous stability.)

We know that we can't go home again, but what is the cost to our society of holding few things or nothing sacred? To profane what might otherwise be holy is to descend to the level of a nihilist. If there is no objective basis for moral beliefs or a system of morality, we are lost. It is to say that one value system is as good as another. We know from experience that this is patently untrue. Terrorists have a belief system and set of values. Do we really think that their system is as good as ours? It is time to object, "Nonsense!" If we neither revere nor respect anyone or anything, we are kidding ourselves. There will come a time when such standards will boomerang on us. We all worship something. Our behaviors and checkbooks will usually reveal the objects of our veneration. But what if all we really worship is the lack of standards, the unprepossessing freedom to do whatever we want whenever we want? What if we worship the right to consume, at ever more sophisticated levels? Companies consume other companies in countless mergers and acquisitions, and whether we can or cannot afford it, we all must have the latest technological gadgets. We wink at each other as we hold loosely to traditional values of thrift, faith, and the preservation of the family, recognizing in them the cramped moorings that will prevent us, like Icarus, from spreading our wings and flying off into the sun. Yet if the only thing left sacred is to hold nothing sacred, then really, what do we stand for? I believe that as a people, we are seeking a common moral compass and anchor, but as we engage one another, we are still trying to agree on terms!

(3) The Tension Between Legality and Morality—This theme has even more direct implications for the trends in labor relations that we are discussing here. Bell argues that market concepts and legal rights have come to dominate our thinking in the early twenty-first century. Bell goes on to say that the social and moral realm has continued to lose out to the rights of the economic shareholder. The shareholder moves in and out of a company based solely on financial returns. Stakeholders, those who are likely to have a long-term interest in an organization are likely to discover that their moral rights and boundaries have been overlooked (284–285).

Is Bell oversimplifying the current context in the Western capitalist nations? Let the reader decide. What the author stated in 1996 is still true in 2016. The interests of business and capital are well represented by lobbyists in congress. Although human resource professionals may be able to act as agents on behalf of the employee stakeholder, it might still be argued that it is the tenets of labor relations law, institutionalized in the right to organize, that has the most potential for protecting the interests of employees.

Employees in nonunion shops do have protections under the law, but these protections are mediated through the human resource agent who owes their job to management and cannot advocate for employees in the same way that a union steward can advocate for union employees. In the union setting, there is an institutional framework, collective bargaining that protects the rights of both managers and employees to bargain in good faith. The very structure of detailed rules and procedures ensures that no party, stakeholder, or interest group will be able to act arbitrarily to advance their own interests.

I am no apologist for unions. They can work for good or ill when the organization and its stakeholder complex need to move with agility. Neither, though, am I an apologist for HR vice-presidents who must bridge the law, employee interests, and goals of organization and unit performance. They have a tough job with plenty of dilemmas to manage. Wall Street partners who wish to be left unfettered to maximize profits, seem to need fewer friends. I am an apologist for the lone individual who is left to balance out the ideological perspectives and pragmatics of the four schools. They need to be armed with broad educational perspectives and to be well trained. The world is a dangerous place when you hold on too tightly to an integrated set of half-truths.

The Rights of Individuals in Retreat

The sociopolitical context in this country has moved from New Deal economics, through postwar protected markets, to globalism and global economics. Global constraints to trade have dissolved, capitalist business values have proliferated, and our original social agenda, "Give me your tired, your poor, your huddled masses yearning to breathe free, the wretched refuse of your teeming shore. Send these, the homeless, tempest-tossed to me. I lift my lamp beside the golden door!" (Lazarus 1883), seems now to be at risk. Donald Trump, the billionaire and Republican presidential candidate in 2016, wants to send all illegal immigrants and Syrian refugees back home.[1] The Industrial Relations frame, upon which our labor laws and policies are based, has been in retreat for decades. On the path to neo-classical prosperity (while suffering nations around the world hope to benefit from the American dream of democratic freedom and economic prosperity), we have begun to wonder whether we can afford our "tired, poor, and huddled masses, yearning to breathe free." They have become a social embarrassment. We worry that they are affecting our ability to attract tourist dollars. We want the unemployed to get jobs; yet have no jobs to give them.

---

1   McCarthy, T. (2015, Aug 27). Donald Trump wants to deport 11,000,000 migrants: Is that even possible? Retrieved from http://www.theguardian.com

Is the Era of Compromise Over?

In this context, are not the industrial relations values of efficiency, equity, and voice (Budd 2008) hopelessly outdated? Although we deny that there is a managerial class (critical IR school), MBA programs have proliferated over the last few decades, and middle class managers and professionals want to preserve the economic gains they have achieved during periods of major economic expansion. These have occurred—with exceptions—into the twenty-first century. Talk of unions is wedded, disparagingly, with entitlements, unwieldy cost structures, and (not to be forgotten) liberal whining. Alongside this, we have all witnessed the transformation and almost-demise of General Motors as it struggled to be competitive with a massive legacy labor cost. Alongside global expansion we witness the paradox and irony of global contraction. Ideas and philosophies seem to have failed us. We still have a democratic system of government, but we are in danger of conceptually polarizing our thought models. We cannot seem to think outside of the boxes of political left and right. Groupthink is in the ascendance (Janis 1982). There has been a reaction to the increased complexity we have experienced in our world and an apparent loss of control over economic factors. Ideologies replace fact-based compromise in government. Ideologies become decision premises instead of guiding frameworks. In regard to raising our borrowing ceiling against the national debt, should we cut costs, increase tax revenues, or both (or neither)? Those who question the legitimacy of government and its prerogatives almost always say, "Cut costs with no new taxes!" Those who see government and its socio-economic interventions as the solution, say, "Avoid drastic cuts in government programs and raise taxes." Those who look for people and principles to execute say, "Government is the enemy and our president the Anti-Christ."

The industrial relations frame, shaken in debt ceiling crises to the point of bargaining impasse (Budd 2008, 338) seems irrelevant to many Americans when applied to the context of individual organizations or industries. The principle of individual freedom is used to undercut an equally important American principle of community responsibility for the whole.

Partnering for Common Ground

Having called the current context into question, in the remainder of this chapter, I will argue that (1) There is still a place for the industrial relations model (and maybe even unions) in the United States; (2) a mixed-motive framework for understanding how public, private, and non-profit sectors can be made more effective still has great untapped potential. Working together, through stakeholder partnerships, various sectors and interest groups can strategically manage a plurality of joint interests, without polarizing their positions. In a global context of loosely coupled organizations, they are uniquely positioned to do that. If the industrial relations model still has a place here, the best place to model it is in these partnering relationships.

As I have attempted to show, at the highest levels of the federal government, contention, unity, and compromise are the name of the game. As with elected officials, public sector organizations serve multiple constituencies and interest groups. Consider that organizations are tools of their owners (Thompson 2003) and that taxpayers own public sector organizations,

The taxpayer is also investor, customer, manager, and employee (among others). There is a binding thread of unity and potential influence here. We as voters have our hands in the mix because we elect the individuals who will make decisions and legislate regarding the fates or futures of public sector agencies. There are administrators, employees, unions, direct customers of products and services, community groups, boards, and government watchdog groups, to name just a few.

Public service organizations, funded mostly by taxpayers, do not have the luxury of treating any of their interest groups like objects to be moved on an organizational chessboard in the interests of strategy and the bottom-line. Unlike the private sector, they cannot easily leave the area in search of more favorable social and economic conditions. Public sector organizations are embedded in their communities. They are part of them. Each of the stakeholder groups have their own requirements and expectations and are capable of exerting political pressures on the organization, because it is always a bit unclear whose interests are most important. Many group interests overlap, and some individuals play multiple roles within different groups. Having both feet in different camps attenuates the sharpness of conflicts and strengthens ambiguity of context. The interests themselves are up for grabs, and the battle for organizational stakes and resources is often fought at the pettiest of levels. In this context, latticed conflicts, alliances, and just plain entanglements emerge to be arbitrated by administrators and boards, often in public forums like open meetings where issues of policy and procedure will be debated![2]

If government and its prerogatives is a political lightening rod today, it is significant that public sector unions have grown from their beginnings in the 1960s to the point where their members constitute 35.2% of the total public sector work force (Bureau of Labor Statistics 2016). In contrast, the private sector union population dropped from 35% in 1955 to only 6.7% today. Across the board, 11.1% of all wage and salary workers are unionized. It is not because nonunion employees do not have grievances that remain unaddressed. Budd (2008) points out that in private sector organizations, there is a representation gap of forty percent (23 24). That means over a third of all private sector employees express a desire for unions in their own organization. In other words, in research findings, when they speak candidly with anonymity guaranteed and no reason to lie, they are saying they would like about the same union representation level as the public sector already has. It is management policy that holds them back. Whether they know it or not, they recognize implicitly that organizations are mixed motive settings, that there is a diversity of interests, and that these interests will, at least part of the time, express themselves in an adversarial manner.

In spite of common opinion and the desires of the private sector, we have not left the issue of union representation behind. It is simply that management has had its way in so many cases, the national discourse on the topic has shifted, or that some private sector organizations have pursued a progressive HR-framed agenda that has produced fruitful

---

2   The author has consulted to organizations at the Federal, State, and County levels. He has also consulted to and worked for academic institutions (including teaching hospitals) that were arguably even more complex.

results. There is nothing wrong with that. Note, though, that many workers are saying that they do not feel adequately represented. That means that they do not believe their rights and fundamental interests are being adequately addressed!

A good example of where the representation gap has turned to action is in a major research university in the Midwest. In 2015, the adjunct faculty approved a unionization vote. In a private university located in the same town, the same stakeholder group of adjunct faculty, declined unionization by a narrow margin. These are professionals in higher education, many with Ph. D.'s. These results demonstrate that stakeholder differences and conflicts of interests cannot be entirely suppressed by enlightened HR practices.

A final point: Unions and managers deliberated around a specific range of issues, and have an institutional framework to contain that conflict—including mediation and arbitration—both parties seem to get things done. No, the process may not be as quick as downsizing, but it is worth noting that even in mergers and acquisition, there is a time of study, thoughtful analysis, and scenario thinking called due diligence. Negotiating a contract and living by the framework and rules contained in the contracts, is a conflict management tool and process. Petty differences are more easily resolved and major issues are brought to the negotiating table.

The Case for Partnerships

Institutionalizing conflict management through a process of labor management and employee engagement has many advantages for today's organizations in an era of instability and change:

1. With such a structure and framework, it is more likely that resistance to organizational changes will be surfaced, addressed, and channeled rather than driven underground, ignored, or left to languish.

2. As long as the players do not limit themselves to the routines, habits, and conflict resolution strategies of the past, sacred cows (inhibiting cultural assumptions and beliefs) can be jointly explored and experiments to improve effectiveness can be undertaken.

3. The acceptable limits of these conversations can be worked out, tracked, and modified in the light of ongoing experience and external change.

If, for the moment, one accepts the possibility that this could or should happen, without dismissing the ideas as impractical, then one would be duplicating this consultant's experience with labor-management partnerships. Both the adversarial and the collaborative dynamic are integrated into one social innovation.

The Politics of Leading Change

In my consulting experience with both private and public sectors, when this works, that is, when a true 50–50 partnership for change is created, a number of factors tend to be involved: First, there is parity in the arena of power. I can strongly influence you to do something you would otherwise not do. Without this joint leverage, it is too easy for one side of the partnership to withdraw when the going gets tough. This is really not so different from mergers and acquisitions when one organization is far more powerful and well-resourced than the other. When the merger has to be forced and actual post-merger integration fails to occur, important relationships are damaged, a variety of corporate stakeholders lose, and resources are diminished. Power discrepancies tend to build on a foundation of both disrespect and distrust, and it is the rare organization that can overcome this problem. Where unions still might exist, one cannot assume that simply because there is a binding collective bargaining contract that this constitutes power parity. A better measure is that both sides have a history of wins and compromises with each other and that therefore each has something to gain by partnering (this could even be said of nonunion partnerships). If either party has suffered severe and protracted losses as a result of previous collective bargaining episodes, it is probably not possible to create joint-ness absent considerable repair work being done with a skilled third party who can help both groups put the past aside in their search for common ground. It helps if there is an external threat or opportunity for the firm that tends to alert both labor and management that a new approach might make sense. As I mentioned in my chapter on impasse, people often do not transform until they face a new challenge that bankrupts their old organizations and practices. The sooner this happens, the better. Otherwise people are likely to trust in their own knowledge base and character as their best resource for the future. They will fail to see that there is something flawed about their thinking.

A good example of this was a Fortune 500 company I worked with that was planning to shut down one of its plants because of excess capacity. The plant had had very antagonistic labor relations during the previous period, with two bitter strikes in four years. The parent company informed management and union leaders that if they wanted to guarantee their future, they had better find a way to get along in the sense that we imply by partnership. The parent company gave them the option of initiating a partnership prototype for the corporation that the parent company would help to fund. This union had power parity, and both union and management saw a common outside enemy. It is not common today for such conditions to exist in many private sector organizations. External threats to organizational survival certainly do exist—now more than ever—but where unions exist, strikes tend to be a less commonly employed tool for a number of very good reasons, which I won't go into here. In the public sector, strikes are often illegal (Budd 2008, 289, 310).

Whatever the situation, the question of power parity remains. As private sector union membership has gone down across the board, the context for power parity has shifted. Even if a particular union is strong in relation to its management counterparts, the general trend in the society toward loss of union power and influence in the private sector may tend to make management more reluctant to partner with employee groups where any kind of adversarial relationship has existed. Corporations will be likely to see their internal management practices as enlightened and part of their competitive advantage. Also by searching worldwide for new labor pools and building new facilities where it is cheapest and most convenient, the company is in a position to reduce power parity by voting with its feet. Buy U.S. is a loyal thing for American citizens to do, but it is unlikely to significantly reduce the trend toward the loss of overall private sector union representation unless that trend has already bottomed out.

A Framework for Workplace Democracy in New Clothes

Cynthia Eastlund (2013) a professor at New York University School of Law, has contended that unions have lost the contest in the private sector but argues that workplace democracy can be decoupled from the industrial relation frame and placed squarely within the HR frame of reference. She cites diversity and inclusion as the likely rubric to cover these types of power sharing. As stated earlier, diversity and inclusion can be strategic agents of competitive advantage that shift a work culture in the direction of creativity and innovation. We also noted that knowledge sharing and moral/ethical leadership are essential for effective organizational processes and outcomes. Workplace democracy is only one step farther, but it is sometimes a big step.

Even with diversity and inclusion, this author argues that the organization needs to harness the twin engines of conflict and collaboration, in a holistic way, for the greater good. Finding a way to do that can be sticky. Employees can view participation in strategic planning or strategic alignment as a top-down driven activity. Democracy means that we all get an opportunity to attempt to influence one another and to at least have a vote on the significant outcomes. The HR/OD template says to work toward consensus, in teams, but the demands of today's modern corporation sometimes drive those activities out. As noted earlier, by the author, "we don't have the time for this kind of 'buy-in'" is a common viewpoint. Different interests, expectations, and desired outcomes will continue to coexist. The question is whether diversity and inclusion can up the ante for full-blown expression of everyone's interest and then tie everyone to performance and a shared institutional vision. This goes beyond appreciative activities to the recognition and management of institutional politics and conflict as either enablers or obstacles to unity of purpose. As noted earlier, there is no easy way to face our organizational demons.

With all sectors facing conditions of scarcity and constraint, all organizational stakeholders should (1) consider each other as potential partners (acting accordingly), (2) throwaway outworn models, prejudices, and behaviors, (3) reach across organizational boundaries to test assumptions and embrace differences, and (4) take the risk of open inquiry that leads to learning!

DISCUSSION QUESTIONS FOR YOU

1. If you are a manager with nonexempt or unionized employees reporting to you, why do you think they should trust you? What have you done to empower them lately? If you consider yourself enlightened, give examples of how you learned about partnering from your direct reports.

2. If you are a nonexempt or unionized employee, explain what you would expect to gain or lose if you became a full-blown partner to everyone you work with.

3. In the search for common ground among organization stakeholders do you see any room for approaches outlined in this chapter?

4. Are unionized workers simply looking for a free ride? Explain. (In answering this question, you are only permitted to generalize from your experience. No piggybacking on far left or far right political ideologies—the fringes of the Democratic or Republican parties.)

REFERENCES

Argyris, C. (1990). *Overcoming organizational defenses: Facilitating organizational change.* Upper Saddle River, NJ: Prentice Hall.

Bell, D. (1996). *The cultural contradictions of capitalism* (20th anniversary ed.). New York, NY: Basic Books.

Budd, J. W. (2008). *Labor relations: Striking a balance* (2nd ed.). New York: McGraw-Hill.

Donald N. Levine (Ed.). (1971). *Georg Simmel: On individuality and social forms.* Chicago, IL: University of Chicago Press.

Canby, V. (1992, December 25). Hoffa (1992): Review/Film; Big Labor's Maser of Manipulation. *The New York Times.* Retrieved from http://movies.nytimes.com/movie/review?res=9E0 CE2DD133AF936A15751C1A964958260

Estlund, C. (2013). *Citizens of the corporation? Workplace democracy in a post-union Era. New York University Public Law and Legal Theory Working Papers.* Paper 442. Retrieved from http://lsr.nellco.org/cgi/viewcontent.cgi?article=1445&context=nyu_plltwp

Gergen, D. (2001). *Eyewitness to power.* New York, NY: Simon & Schuster.

Janis, I. L. (1982). *Psychological studies of policy decisions and fiascoes* (2nd ed.). Farmington Hills, MI: Cengage Learning.

John F. Kennedy (January 20, 1961). Inaugural Address. Retrieved from http://en.wikipedia. org/wiki/Ask_not_what_your_country_can_do_for_you#Notable_passages

Lasch, C. (1979). *The culture of narcissism: American life in an age of diminishing expectations.* New York, NY: Norton.

Lazarus, E. (1883). The New Colossus. Retrieved from http://en.wikipedia.org/wiki/ The_New_Colossus

Madison, J., Hamilton, A., & Jay, J. (1987). *The federalist papers.* London, UK: Penguin.

Peters, T. J. & Waterman, R. H. (2004). *In search of excellence.* New York, NY: HarperBusiness.

Salinger, J. D. (2001). *Catcher in the rye.* New York, NY: 2001.

Sherman, J. (1993). *In the rings of Saturn.* New York, NY: Oxford University Press.

Taylor, F. W. (2011). *The principles of scientific management.* Seattle, WA: CreateSpace.

Thompson, J. D. (2003). *Organizations in action: Social science bases of administrative theory.* Piscataway, NJ: Transaction Publishers.

Weber, M. (2008). *The protestant ethic and the spirit of capitalism.* Miami, FL: BN Publishing.

Authenticity, "blossoms," impasse, psychological dilemmas, bankruptcy, mapping, limits and contractions, moral management, organizational grace, diversity and inclusion, differences that make a difference, labor relations. Key words and themes that make-up this book! What ties them together? Who cares? I do. I am an author who feels deeply about life and the nature of things. I care about people, their organizations, their lives.

Back to the Future

In this book, I have argued that executives and managers need a change of heart and consciousness if we are to create something lasting and noble out of collective enterprise. I am both hopeful and doubtful about the outcome of all of our efforts in organizations. It is not just because managers tend to objectify people, at times, to gain control. They do, but that is overly simplistic. I am not so naive as to assume that employees are without power and prerogatives. As I have tried to demonstrate in this book, there are formal positions that convey power and legitimacy in every organization, but there is also lot of organizational, institutional, and even state power that is up for grabs. We may all gain power and influence to the extent that we are able to step outside of our pet frames of references, investigate what we don't understand with fresh eyes, and give up the quest for control through either action or analysis, alone. It often leads to fruitless arguments and dead-ends. For example, Charles Krauthammer, Washington Post Opinion Writer, recently interpreted the "failure of the unions to recall Wisconsin Gov. Scott Walker (R)—the first such failure in U.S. history—[as] ... the Icarus moment of government-union power.

Wax wings melted, there's nowhere to go but down"[1]. Just as President Reagan was touted as busting the private sector unions in the American Aircraft Controllers' debacle, now the failure of a recall is being framed as the death-knell of our country's union movement. Subsequent articles tossed the bombshell back and forth across the analytical tennis net, trying to determine what to make of it[2]. One thing, of course, was certain: The frame was the key! If one already had an ideological dislike of unions, then they were bound to be corrupt wasters of the taxpayer's money. If one had an affinity for the union principle, one back-pedaled to find a ray of hope in this all-too-tragic state of affairs. The context was also the key:

"If all those well-paying blue collar jobs hadn't flown the coop over the last few decades, if the global melt-down hadn't occurred, if entitlements hadn't gone through the roofs, if we didn't need somebody to blame for everything that has gone wrong in this country over the last five decades, if President Obama had not gotten Obamacare through Congress, if people were not just plain suffering, why then the unions must have had a right to exist [what I thinks going-on]! Government being the enemy, of course, and public sector employees, 'pigs at the public trough,' you can't really blame us for wanting to take away their bargaining rights! The federal government is the enemy! Just let the market mechanisms operate! The system is the enemy! Hey, hey, what d'ya say, take that ball the other way!"

The world has changed. Yet we are still trying to apply thought models from a world that no longer exists. We want to avoid the

---

1   Washington Post, June 8, 2012, ¶ 1
2   E. J. Dionne, Jr., Michael Gerson, Charles Lane, Greg Sargent, June 8, 2012

necessary pain and uncertainty that goes with an era of tumultuous change. Even this author has presumptuously tried to catch up by suggesting that the union principle might still have some viability in a world now seemingly dominated by Fox News, the IPhone, Facebook, and continually stepping back from the economic brink. We live in a time of fear, awe, hope, and wonder. An age of complexity calls for complex thinking patterns coupled with the conceptual naiveté of a child. We must be ready to jettison models and metaphors that no longer help to explain the complex reality in which we find ourselves, and substitute new ones. When those new ones begin to take on the power of dogma, we must jettison those.

To return to the essential premise of this book—"Human beings, being themselves and making responsible choices to think and act with integrity, can enrich the organizational environment and create a climate of greater choice for everyone. The onus is on individual decision and choice, not top management and the executive team" (see page 11 of this book). The reader will need to decide whether I have marshaled sufficient evidence to support the premise. If, no matter where you are in your organization, you are now taking increased responsibility for thought leadership, better informed decision making, and executive action within your sphere of influence, I will have accomplished my purpose.

I have attempted to counter some traditional streams of consciousness with counterintuitive flashpoints. Finishing this book has been difficult because the rapid flow of events forces a continuous update of facts and perspectives. Nevertheless, at some point one must draw a boundary around a volume and say, "I have said all I want to say." This is not a timely article that can quickly be followed by another timely article (should events supersede themselves). Many of the topics in this book are timeless. I speculate on matters that are conceptually discrete, yet interwoven into a holistic tapestry extending backward into the past and forward into an unfathomable future. Let the book speak for itself. I welcome dialogue on statements I have made and blog entries on my website. I want to challenge and be challenged. Thank you for buying the book and reading it. Let me know what you think…

REFERENCES

Charles Krauthammer, E. J. Dionne, Jr., Michael Gerson, Charles Lane, Greg Sargent (June 8, 2012). *Washington Post Online.* Retrieved from

file:///Users/jeffhaldeman/Desktop/Charles%20Krauthammer:%20What%20 Wisconsin%20means%20-%20The%20Washington%20Post.html

http://www.washingtonpost.com/opinions/public-employee-unions-should-learn- from-their-wisconsin-defeat/2012/06/06/gJQA4frlJV_story.html

http://www.washingtonpost.com/opinions/michael-gerson-democrats-are-playing-with-dynamite/2012/06/06/gJQAwDdbJV_story.html

http://www.washingtonpost.com/opinions/wisconsins-lessons-for-the-left-and-the-right/2012/06/06/gJQAtxeulV_story.html

http://www.washingtonpost.com/blogs/post-partisan/post/democracy-wins-in-wisconsin/2012/06/06/gJQAzdJKJV_blog.html

http://www.washingtonpost.com/blogs/plum-line/post/a-wake-up-call-for-dems-labor-and-the-left/2012/06/05/gJQAfKBQHV_blog.html

GENERAL REFERENCES

Haldeman, J. T. (2003). *The psychological dilemmas of leadership.* Paper presented at the National Conference of the Academy of Business Administration, Las Vegas, NV.

Haldeman, J. T. (2004). *A multi-disciplinary framework for knowledge management.* Paper presented at the National Conference of the Academy of Business Administration, Las Vegas, NV.

Haldeman, J. T. (2012). The learning organization: From dysfunction to grace. *Journal of Management and Marketing Research.* 5, 85–93.

CPSIA information can be obtained
at www.ICGtesting.com
Printed in the USA
FSHW012018221019
63280FS